CONTACT
with GOD

Jose,
The key to freedom
has no keys.
Raquel
7/9/21

CONTACT
with GOD

Retreat
Conferences

ANTHONY DE MELLO

Image/Doubleday
New York   London   Toronto   Sydney   Auckland

AN IMAGE BOOK
PUBLISHED BY DOUBLEDAY
a division of Random House, Inc.

IMAGE, DOUBLEDAY, and the portrayal of a deer drinking from a stream are registered
trademarks of Random House, Inc.

Book design by Donna Sinisgalli

The Library of Congress has cataloged the 1991 Loyola Press edition as follows:
De Mello, Anthony, 1931–1987
   Contact with God: retreat conferences/Anthony de Mello.
     p. cm.
   1. Jesuits—Spiritual life. 2. Retreats. 3. Spiritual exercises. 4. Spiritual life—
Catholic authors. I. Title.
BX3703.D46 1991
269'.6—dc20   91–30524
                                                        CIP

ISBN 0-385-50994-4
Copyright © 1991 by Loyola Press
All Rights Reserved

PRINTED IN THE UNITED STATES OF AMERICA

Contents

Preface to the American Edition

Contact with God was published posthumously by Gujarit Sahitya Prakash, a Jesuit press in India. In undertaking an American edition, the editors had a dilemma of sorts; for example, whether to generalize and formalize the text, or to leave it more or less as delivered orally to a male—and Indian Jesuit—religious audience. In deference to Father de Mello, it appeared the better course was to follow the original text where it served, leaving the reader to adjust to his spoken style and to accept a number of informalities. His paraphrasing of Scripture and some absence of attribution where texts are quoted are examples. It being a posthumous publication, the usual recourse of querying the author was, naturally, not possible. Outside of quotations American spellings are used, and inclusive language was employed where the text permitted it.

Joseph F. Downey, S.J.
Editorial Director
Loyola University Press

◁ Foreword

Those who were familiar with Tony de Mello in his lifetime know and still remember that his ministry went through several distinct stages, corresponding partly to the needs of the people he served but also to the demands of an inner development. Externally, one could perceive successively the spiritual director, the therapist, the guru; internally, a close friend has spoken of "the progression of values from holiness through love to freedom."

Obviously, these values are not mutually exclusive; nor were the stages compartmentalized. There was not only continuity but a certain unity in the various roles he assumed. In fact, one might say that he was first and last a spiritual director in the great Christian tradition. Further, it could be argued that the ultimate reason why he remained popular to the end, when some had misgivings about the way he was going, was that he never outlived his beginnings and always came across as an incomparable guide to closer contact with God.

And so we come to this posthumous publication: a transcript of his retreat conferences, which he himself carefully edited but never released. There is no answer to why he did not make them available; or to what he would think of the present venture. The incontestable fact is that many people of all sorts will be very happy to have these notes.

The text is reproduced just as Tony left it; only a title has been provided, and some slips were corrected—though there was a suggestion favoring revision. The style is somewhat old-fashioned, the content not altogether post-conciliar, the language quite sexist.[1] This last flaw, regarded as unpardonable today, could be excused because he was originally addressing Jesuits. But there is hardly any reference to the Ignatian Spiritual Exercises, which were presumably dealt with in private interviews. The subject of the talks can be summed up in the classical Three Fundamental Principles: prayer, penance and the love of Christ. The style is typical of Tony: forceful.

That is how he always was; he did not impose himself but irresistibly invited us to share in his experience. In the final phase before his death, it was not clear what he experienced; and his attempts at articulation were not too convincing. But he was always the same Tony. So this book is a sort of homecoming; and it is appropriately timed for the Ignatian Jubilee, which commemorates the birth of Ignatius of Loyola in 1491, and calls on Jesuits and their friends all over the world to enter more deeply into the spiritual legacy of the saint.

For this occasion, Tony de Mello and his retreat conferences have a message, and we find it expressed in a homily he delivered much later, on July 31, 1983:

> We need to sink deep roots into God if we are going to be attuned to the creating Spirit within, if we are going to have the power to love and to be loyal to this Church which will at times oppose and misunderstand us. Only contemplatives can do this. Only they will know how to combine loyalty and obedience with creativity and confrontation. I pray at this Mass that God and history will not find us wanting. I pray that Saint Ignatius will have cause to be proud of us.

Parmananda R. Divarkar, S.J.
Bombay
June 1990

---

[1] We have tried to remedy the problem of noninclusive language in the American edition, see page vii—ed.

1

Receiving the
Holy Spirit

I wish to situate this retreat in the context of the Church and the world today. We have assembled here for a period of silence and prayer and withdrawal at a time when the Church is in crisis and the world in desperate need of peace and development and justice. May we not be rightly accused of escapism? Can we afford the luxury of an eight-day withdrawal when the house is on fire and every available hand is needed to put the fire out?

Are We Escapists?

I want to continue with that comparison. The house is indeed on fire. But too many of us, tragically, have no motivation to put it out; we would rather busy ourselves with our little worlds and little lives. Too many of us are too blind even to notice the fire—we notice only what suits us. And even supposing we are gifted with motivation and proper sight, how many of us lack the strength to work perseveringly on this fire; how many of us lack the wisdom and reflection to find the best and quickest means for putting the fire out? And then there is so much selfishness in the way we set about the task—a selfishness that makes us come in one another's way even when we have good intentions.

The retreat, on the face of it, does seem like a luxury and an escape. But it is the kind of luxury taken by a general who withdraws from the direct line of firing to give himself time to reflect and to come up with a more effective plan of battle. It is the kind of escape that will enable us to strengthen our motivation, to widen our hearts, to sharpen our sight, to energize ourselves to plunge more wholeheartedly into the tasks that God has assigned for us in the world. Dag Hammarskjöld, the mystic who became U.N. Secretary General, was so right when he said in his diary, "In our era the path to holiness necessarily passes through the world of action." We contemplate and pray to re-create ourselves and to act more energetically and more effectively for God's glory and the benefit of the world.

The Greatest Need of the Church

The Church is passing through a period of chaos and crisis. This is *not* necessarily a bad thing. A crisis is a challenge to grow. Chaos precedes creation—provided, and this is a big proviso, the Spirit of God is hovering over it.

The greatest need of the Church today is not new legislation, new theology, new structures, new liturgies—all these without the Holy Spirit are like a dead body without a soul. We desperately need someone to take away our hearts of stone and give us a heart of flesh; we need a fresh infusion of enthusiasm and inspiration and courage and spiritual strength. We need to persevere in our task without discouragement or cynicism, with new faith in the future and in the people we work for. In other words, we need a fresh outpouring of the Holy Spirit.

To put this more concretely, we need *people* who are charged with the Holy Spirit. The Spirit works through people. Salvation comes through people. "There was a man sent from God whose name was John," we read at the dawn of Christ's coming. A *person*, not a plan, not a blueprint, not a message. "Unto us a child is born, unto us a son is given"—God saved us, not through a "plan of salvation" but through a human being, Jesus Christ, a man who was mighty in the Spirit. The Holy Spirit does not come down upon buildings but upon people; it is people he anoints, not blueprints; he circulates in the hearts and spirits of human beings, not in the latest machinery.

So to say that the Church's most desperate need is for a fresh infusion of the Holy Spirit is to say that the Church needs a whole army of spirit-filled people. That is why we are making this retreat. We have come here in the hope that we shall become spirit-filled people. We have withdrawn with the attitude and the expectation with which the apostles withdrew to the cenacle before Pentecost.

How to Get the Holy Spirit

There's nothing more certain than this: The Holy Spirit is not produced by any efforts of our own. He cannot be "merited." There is absolutely nothing we can *do* to get him. He is a pure gift of the Father.

The problem we face is the problem the apostles faced. They, like us, were in need of the Holy Spirit for their apostolate. Jesus gave them instructions on how to receive the Holy Spirit. He said,

> You must, *wait* for the promise made by my Father, about which you have heard me speak: John, as you know, baptized with water, but you will be baptized with the Holy Spirit, and within the next few days. . . . You will *receive power* when the Holy Spirit comes upon you; and you will bear witness for me in Jerusalem, and all over Judaea and Samaria, and away to the ends of the earth.

Jesus said, "Wait." We can't produce the Spirit. We can only *wait* for him to come. And this is something our poor human nature finds very hard to do in our modern world. We cannot wait.

We cannot sit still. We are too restless, too impatient. We have to be up and about. We'd rather undertake many hours of hard labor than endure the pain of waiting in stillness for something that is beyond our control; something whose time of arrival we do not know. But wait we must; so we wait and wait and wait—but nothing happens (or rather, nothing we can perceive with our unrefined spiritual sight), so we tire of waiting and praying. We are more at home "working for God" and so we drown ourselves in activity again. Yet the Spirit is given only to those who wait; those who expose their hearts day after day to God and his Word in prayer, those who invest hours and hours in what seems a sheer waste of time to our production-oriented minds.

We read in Acts 1:4: "While Jesus was in their company he told them not to leave Jerusalem. 'You must wait,' he said, 'for the promise of my Father.' " Do not leave Jerusalem. Once again, resist the urge to be up and doing before you are freed from the compulsion to act; the urge to communicate to others what you yourself have not yet experienced. Once the Spirit has come, "You will bear witness for me in Jerusalem . . . and to the ends of the earth." But not before, or you will be lying witnesses—or, at best, you will be pushers, not apostles. Pushers are insecure people who have a compulsion to convince others, so that they themselves will be less insecure.

Jesus said, "You will receive power." Receive is an accurate word! Jesus does not expect us to produce power, because this kind of power cannot be produced no matter how hard we try. It can only be received. I am reminded here of a woman who said, "I have attended dozens of seminars at which I have picked up at least a hundred beautiful ideas. What I need now is not more beautiful ideas. I need the *power* to put at least one of those ideas into action!" This is the reason why a retreat is not like a seminar: there are no lectures, no group discussions; there is a lot of silence and prayer and exposure to God.

What to Do Concretely: An Attitude

For tomorrow morning's prayer and, if you wish, for the whole of tomorrow's prayer, I want to recommend to you an attitude and a practice. The attitude is one of great expectation. St. John of the Cross says that people receive from God as much as they expect from God. If you expect little you will generally receive little. If you expect much, you will receive much. Do you need a miracle of grace in your life? Then you must expect a miracle to happen. How many miracles have you experienced in your personal life? None? That is only because you weren't expecting any. God never lets you down when your expectations of him are high; he may keep you waiting, or he may come at once, or he may come suddenly and unexpectedly like a "thief at night," to use Jesus' expression. But come he surely will if you are expecting him to come.

Someone has rightly said that *the* sin against the Holy Spirit is to no longer believe that he can change the world, to no longer believe that he can change me. This is a more dangerous kind of atheist than those who say, "God does not exist," for, while telling themselves that they believe in God, they have blinded themselves into a practical atheism of which they are hardly aware. They say, "God can no longer change me. He doesn't have the will and the power to transform me, to raise me from the dead. I know, because I have tried everything. I've made so many retreats, prayed so fervently, had so much good will—but nothing has happened, just nothing." The God of these people is, for all practical purposes, a dead God—not the God who by raising Jesus from the dead has shown us that nothing is impossible to him. Or, to use the lovely expression of St. Paul who speaks of Abraham in Romans 4; he is the God in whom Abraham put his faith,

the God who makes the dead live and summons things that are not yet in existence as if they already were. When hope seemed hopeless, his (Abraham's) faith was such that he became "father

of many nations," in agreement with the words which had
been spoken to him: "Thus shall your posterity be." Without
any weakening of faith he contemplated his own body, as good
as dead (for he was about a hundred years old), and the deadness of Sarah's womb, and never doubted God's promise, but
strong in faith he gave honour to God, in the firm conviction
of his power to do what he had promised.

What to Do Concretely: A Practice

I suggest that you read Luke 11:1–13 sedulously. Read it again
and again and ask yourself: What is my response to Jesus' words,
"How much more will the heavenly Father give the Holy Spirit to
those who ask him!"

Wait till you feel faith enough in Jesus' words to really ask for
the Holy Spirit in full confidence. And then, *ask!* Ask repeatedly, ask
earnestly, ask increasingly, even shamelessly, like that man knocking
at his friend's door at midnight, refusing to take No for an answer.
There are some things we can ask God for only with the proviso, "If
it be your will." There's no such proviso here. It *is* clearly God's will,
his clear *promise*, to give you the Spirit. What is lacking is not his de
sire to give you the Spirit, but (a) your faith that he means to give
the spirit to you and (b) constant asking on your part.

So don't hesitate to invest a lot of time in just asking and asking tirelessly. Say something like "Give us the Spirit of Christ,
Lord, for we are your children;" or, "Come, Holy Spirit, Come,
Holy Spirit." Any ejaculation will do: say it slowly, with attention,
with earnestness. Say it a hundred times, a thousand times, ten
thousand times.

Or ask without words. Just look up to heaven or at the taber-
nacle in silence and in a spirit of supplication. If you are alone in
your room, you may want to make this supplication not just with
your eyes, but with your whole body—raising your hands to
heaven, perhaps, or prostrating yourself repeatedly on the floor.

This may not be "meditation." It may bring you no great insights or "lights." But this is *prayer*. And the Holy Spirit is given in answer to earnest *prayer*, not in response to cleverly thought out meditations. Pray, not just for yourself, but for all of us—for the whole group. Don't say just "Give me," say also "Give *us*."

And, if you wish your prayer to have its maximum power and intensity, do what the apostles did when they waited for the Spirit before Pentecost—pray with Mary. The saints assure us that it was never known that anyone who sought her intercession or fled to her protection was left unaided. You can make this experience of the saints your own by having recourse to Mary in all of your needs. Then you will know this not because of what the saints say but because of what you have personally felt and experienced. Consecrate this retreat to Mary, the Mother of Jesus. Seek her blessing as you embark upon it. You will notice what a difference it makes.

Finally, here are some psalms that may help you to put into words your petitionary prayer for the Spirit tomorrow: Psalm 4:[1] Only the light of your face can bring us happiness. Psalm 6: But you, O Lord . . . how long? Each night I weep. Return, Lord . . . how long? Psalm 12: How long will you hide your face? Psalm 15: My happiness lies in you alone. Psalm 23: (second half) Let him enter, the king of glory. Psalm 26: This is one thing I ask of the Lord. For this I long . . . One thing I long for—to live in the house of the Lord. It is your face, O Lord, that I seek. Psalm 32: Our soul is waiting for the Lord. In him do our hearts find joy. Psalm 37: Lord, you know all my longing; my groans are not hidden from you. Psalm 41: My soul is thirsting for God. My tears have become my bread, by day, by night. Psalm 42: Why are you cast down? Hope in God. Psalm 62: My body pines for you like dry, weary land without water. On you I muse all through the night. Psalm

[1] The numbering for the Psalms that Father de Mello uses follows the Hebrew, not the Septuagint version, and so is different from most Catholic editions.

120: My soul is longing for the Lord more than the watchman for daybreak. Psalm 136: By the rivers of Babylon there we sat and wept remembering Zion.

You may want to fasten upon one or other of these lines from the Psalms and pour your heart out to God in the words that God himself has given to us with which to address him. They will have the power to give you faith and obtain for you what you are asking for.

2

The Apostle's
Retreat

I want to start this conference with a question that is possibly in the minds of some of you. It is no longer the custom in many quarters to make a silent retreat—or even to make a retreat at all. Something more in the nature of a seminar or a refresher course on theology or scripture seems more relevant to our needs. We are apostles by vocation, not cloistered contemplatives. Our vocation demands that we *act*, not be still; *speak*, not be silent. So it is, perhaps, understandable that some ask, "What sense does a retreat make to an apostle?"

My response to that is; "A retreat is possibly the most *apostolic* thing an apostle can do. There is, paradoxically, nothing more necessary for apostles than that they withdraw to the desert, that they spend prolonged hours in *listening*, not just talking, that they expose themselves to God and get their spiritual batteries charged before they offer the light to others. In prayer apostles present themselves before God so that God may give them what He wishes him to give to others."

Return to the Source

There is an urgent need today to return to our sources in order to seek renewal. Vatican II has urged us to go back to our roots, to our constitutions and the Gospels, in order to find there the life and the spirit that is peculiarly our own and that must be reinterpreted and lived out in modern times. The return to our sources, however, is not primarily a return to documents. It would be more accurate to speak of a return to our Source, in the singular, for there is only one source of our life as Christians and priests, a living person, Jesus Christ. And this does not involve a return to the past, for Jesus Christ is a person who is living today and can be met today. This is the Source that we must get in touch with and draw all our strength and inspiration from. And this is what a retreat is meant to give you: a chance, not to read books and get fresh insights, but to meet Jesus Christ, if you haven't had that experience as yet; and if you have, to deepen your relationship with him.

The Apostle:
One Who Loves the Master

You are expected, during these days, to give *him* all your time and attention and love, to lavish it all on him, as Mary the sister of Lazarus did with that precious ointment. For the poor we have with us all the year round. But Jesus wants to be known and loved personally, over and above the love we give him in our neighbor and the poor. "Simon, son of John, do you love me more than all else?" "Yes, Lord, you know I love you." "Then feed my lambs." No matter how busy you may be with your Master's work, no matter how important the nature of the task assigned you, your first and chief duty is to have a personal love for the Master. Before Jesus committed the pastoral office to Peter he gave him a screening test. He asked Peter two questions, and both those questions had to do with his own person, not with the flock. The first question was, "Who do you say that I am?" The second, "Do you love me?"

These are the two questions that must resound within our hearts these days as we seek to become more "apostolic." We must hear Jesus say to each of us, "John, Mary, Tom, . . . who do *you* say that I am? In other words, don't just answer with a formula like 'You are the Christ, the Son of the living God.' That was Peter's formula. What formula would you use to describe what I am or who I am *for you?* John, Mary, Tom, . . . do you love me more than all else?" If we wish to be apostles and pastors it is vital for us to deepen our love for Jesus these days so that we can say confidently, "Yes, Lord, you know that I love you indeed."

The Apostle: One Who Has Seen Christ

Before the early Church recognized people as apostles it demanded this of them: that they be people who had seen the Risen Lord. This is partly the reason why Paul had so much difficulty getting his apostolic charism recognized. He insists he is a real apostle, not a bit inferior to the twelve and the other apostles, because he has seen the Risen Lord. "Am I not an apostle?" he says to the Corinthians (1 Corinthians 9:1), "Did I not see Jesus our Lord?"

And he insists that he received his gospel directly from the Lord. He did indeed preach a doctrine that he had received from others. ("First and foremost I handed on to you the facts which had been imparted to me: that Christ died for our sins, in accordance with the scriptures; that he was buried; that he was raised to life on the third day, according to the scriptures and that he appeared to Cephas and afterwards to the Twelve" 1 Corinthians 15.) He got his historical *facts* from others but his *Gospel* and his *commission* to preach the Gospel he received from no one but Jesus himself. Not from the Church, not from the Christian community, not from any authority in the Church, but from Jesus in person. He even seems to have got some of his historical facts from Jesus in person.

> For the tradition which I handed on to you came to me from the Lord himself: that the Lord Jesus, on the night of his arrest,

took bread and, after giving thanks to God, broke it and said: "This is my body, which is for you; do this as a memorial of me."

1 Corinthians 11

Paul will speak boldly of "my gospel" (Romans 2:16). Which of us would dare use an expression like that? Or these bold words from Galatians:

I must make it clear to you, my friends, that the gospel you heard me preach is no human invention. I did not take it over from any man; no man taught it to me; I received it through a revelation of Jesus Christ . . . in his good pleasure God, who had set me apart from birth and called me through his grace, chose to reveal his Son to me and through me, in order that I might proclaim him among the Gentiles. When that happened, without consulting any human being, without going up to Jerusalem to see those who were apostles before me, I went off at once to Arabia, and afterwards returned to Damascus. Three years later I did go up to Jerusalem to get to know Cephas. I stayed with him for a fortnight, without seeing any other of the apostles, except James the Lord's brother. What I write is plain truth; before God I am not lying.

Galatians 1:11–20

Isn't this just the way it ought to be? Apostles are witnesses. They must bear witness to what they themselves have seen and heard if their message is to carry any conviction, just as much as, and even more than, witnesses in court who must witness to what they themselves have seen and heard, if they are to convince; not to what they have picked up from hearsay. How well this point is brought out in the two accounts that Paul gives of his vision of the Risen Lord and his conversion. In Acts 22 he says,

There, a man called Ananias, a devout observer of the Law and well spoken of by all the Jews of the place, came and stood beside me and said, "Saul, my brother, recover your sight." Instantly I recovered my sight and saw him. He went on: "The God of our fathers appointed you to know his will and to *see the Righteous One and to hear his very voice, because you are to be his witness before the world, and testify to what you have seen and heard*."

In Acts 26, it is Jesus himself who says these words to him.

I said, "Tell me, Lord, who you are"; and the Lord replied, "I am Jesus, whom you are persecuting. But now, rise to your feet and stand upright. *I have appeared to you for a purpose: to appoint you my servant and witness, to testify both to what you have seen and to what you shall yet see of me!*"

This is the kind of language the other apostles spoke. John says,

It was there from the beginning; we have heard it; we have seen, it with is of this we tell. Our theme is the word of life. This life was made visible; we have seen it and bear our testimony . . . what we have seen and heard we declare to you, so that you and we together may share in a common life, that life which we share with the Father and his Son Jesus Christ. And we write this in order that the joy of us all may be complete.

1 John 1:1–4

And Peter says,

It was not on tales artfully spun that we relied when we told you of the power of our Lord Jesus Christ and his coming; we saw him with our own eyes in majesty, when at the hands of

God the Father he was invested with honour and glory, and there came to him from the sublime Presence a voice which said, "This is my Son, my Beloved, in whom my favour rests." This voice from heaven we ourselves heard; when it came we were with him on the sacred mountain.

2 Peter 1:16–17

This is no less a test of a true apostle and witness today, two thousand years after Jesus died and rose again, than it was twenty years after his death and resurrection. Every genuine apostle in the history of the Church has measured up to the test. In fact some of them continue to nourish the Church with their doctrine and to influence the life of the Church, men like the Fathers and the Doctors of the Church, precisely because they were men who were in direct touch with Jesus Christ: men who were great contemplatives as Paul and Peter and John were great contemplatives. If to be a contemplative means being in living and constant communion with Jesus the Risen Lord, then how can you be an apostle without being contemplative? And how can you be a contemplative unless you give much time to personal, intimate converse with Christ? This is why we are making a retreat, not a seminar or refresher course.

The Apostle: Someone of the Spirit

We read in Acts 19 that when Paul went to Ephesus he met a group of converts who hadn't even heard there was such a thing as the Holy Spirit. Paul somehow detected this. Then he laid his hands on them and gave them the Holy Spirit. That, after all, is the chief business of the apostle, to give the Holy Spirit to others. This was why they were given the Spirit in the first place; this was to be their specialization, their special contribution to the world. They were to experience the transforming effects of the Spirit in their own hearts first and then make this same transforming power available to others.

Acts 8 tells us that when the apostles heard that Samaria had received the word of God they sent Peter and John down to them to give the new converts the Holy Spirit. That hardly seems fair to Philip, who had done the evangelizing of Samaria. It isn't as if the apostles were the only ones who could give the Spirit to others. This is something every Christian should be able to do, and presumably Philip could have done it quite effectively. But somehow this work seemed most appropriate to the apostles. So Peter and John went down to Samaria. We are told that they

> prayed for the converts, asking that they might receive the Holy Spirit. For until then the Spirit had not come upon any of them. . . . So Peter and John laid their hands on them and they received the Holy Spirit.
>
> Acts 8:15–17

Notice an important detail: they *prayed* before laying hands on those good Samaritans. It was primarily by the power of their prayer that the apostles communicated the Spirit. They themselves had received him only after intensive praying before Pentecost. What more natural than that this should be the way they would normally communicate him to others? Any wonder that they were very reluctant to get immersed in activity that would unduly distract them from this their main task? We hear them say in Acts 6:

> It would be a grave mistake for us to neglect the word of God in order to wait at table. Therefore, friends, choose seven men of good reputation from your number . . . and we will appoint them to deal with these matters, while we devote ourselves to prayer and to the ministry of the Word.

We are living in the age of the hyphenated priest: The priest-worker, the priest-scientist, the priest-artist. We have apostles who are concerned to take up some profession or other as a help to their apostolate. All very well, indeed, provided they keep fully alive what is most characteristic of their vocation as apostles, the ability to communicate the Holy Spirit to others. This is how I would judge the success of our formation programs. At the end of his years of formation I would say to the young priest about to set out on his apostolate, "Do you have the Holy Spirit? Do you feel confident that you can by God's grace, give him to others?" If he says, No, then what is the use of all his formation, of his philosophy and theology and all the expertise he has picked up in languages or homiletics or liturgy or Scripture or the profane sciences or whatever? Of what use is it to the doctor that he is an expert in literature or any other subject, if he is weak in medicine?

Our young priest may be a good theologian. He may even present his theology to others in an attractive way. But the world is not hungering for theology. It is hungry for God. The early Church did not offer people a theology of the Holy Spirit. The theology would come later. First he offered the Holy Spirit himself, the *experience* of His power. The hungry man wants real food, not attractive pictures of food. And a hungry man certainly doesn't want words instead of food. Are our formation programs primarily and centrally geared to equipping our priests not just with words and concepts but with the Holy Spirit? Is this the sole motive behind all the changes we are making in their seminary formation? Is all else rigorously beaten back into second place?

What does it mean to be able to give the Holy Spirit to others? Many things, but boiled down to its essentials it would mean this: to have the experience that you are transforming hearts and lives through the power of your word and the power of your prayer. And of the two, the ability to transform others through the power of prayer is far more important. This is the power that Paul used principally for success in his apostolate. His spoken word doesn't seem to have had much of an effect on people. He willingly accepts the accusation of some of the Corinthians that he was a poor speaker. But the power of his prayer! This he was constantly using. There's barely a letter in which he doesn't say he is constantly praying for his converts. To the Ephesians, for instance, he says,

> I kneel in prayer to the Father from whom every family in heaven and on earth takes its name, that out of the treasures of his glory he may grant you strength and power through his Spirit in your inner being, that through faith Christ may dwell in your hearts in love. With deep roots and firm foundations, may you be strong to grasp, with all God's people, what is the breadth and length and height and depth of the love of Christ, and to know it, though it is beyond knowledge. So you may attain to fullness of being, the fullness of God himself.
>
> Ephesians 3:14–19

Here is Paul seeking to impart to his Christians spiritual gifts (strength, power, faith, love) that no one can impart to another through mere words (for this is something that is beyond words, even beyond all knowledge). And we find him, true apostle that he was, seeking to impart these gifts through the power of his intercessory prayer. There is no other way.

Here, then, is another reason why apostles withdraw to make a retreat: they need to be charged with the Holy Spirit. The Holy Spirit is given to those who watch and pray and wait patiently, those who have the courage to get away from everything and come to grips with themselves and with God in solitude and silence. No wonder every one of the great prophets, indeed Jesus himself, retired to the desert for prolonged periods of silence, praying, fasting, wrestling with the forces of evil. The desert is the furnace where the apostle and the prophet are forged. The desert, not the marketplace. The marketplace is where apostles function. The desert is where they are formed and seasoned and receive their commission and their message for the world, "their" gospel.

The Apostle: Someone of Discernment

Here is another reason why apostles need retreats: the retreat teaches discernment, it helps to create and deepen within our hearts that silence within which the voice of God is heard. And who is in greater need of constantly listening to God's voice than apostles? They must listen so that they may know what to say to others. Even more importantly, they must listen so that they may know where to go, what to do, when to speak, to whom to speak and how. How else will they ever know the will of God?

Apostles are sent on a mission. It is vitally important that they keep constantly in touch with headquarters! How much of what we call our apostolic activity is a great bustle covering up the fact that we are just doing our own will! We haven't taken the time out to purify our hearts of our prejudices and inordinate attachments or aversions, in order to see God's will with unclouded eyes. It is not enough to be full of zeal and goodwill. The pharisees, says St. Paul in Romans 10, had a zeal for God's glory, but it was a misguided zeal and so, far from doing good they were doing positive harm. I am reminded of the priest who once said to me, "Now that I have begun to pray again and see things in the light of the Gospels, I look back with sadness on the many years I have worked for Christ; and I wonder if I have done work for Christ or just given him more work to do in undoing the harm I have done!" What a pity he saw this so late in life; that it took him so long to begin to listen to the voice of God within him before he launched out into action!

When we begin to strain our ears to listen to God's voice we find all kinds of other sounds crowding into our ears: loudest among them are the insistent demands of our own selfish desires; and the most dangerous of these sounds, though not necessarily the loudest, are the whisperings of the angel of darkness, the "prince of this world," as Christ called him, coaxing us on to a path of action that seems to glorify God, for he appears as an angel of light

(2 Corinthians 11:14) but his promptings, if followed, lead to havoc in Christ's kingdom.

That is why apostles need to be people of discernment. Their sight must be clear and their hearing sharp if they are to discern the will of God from their own impulses, the promptings of the Holy Spirit from those of the evil spirit. In Acts, we see the Apostles as people who are constantly attuned to the voice of the Spirit within them precisely because they were men of prayer. In Acts 10, Peter receives the revelation to go to the gentiles; his first response is one of pious horror. But Scripture tells us he was in prayer at that moment, so he was able to overcome his religious prejudices and be open to this unexpected plan of God. If he had not been a man of prayer, if, instead of going up to the terrace to pray that afternoon, he had lost himself in a great bustle of activity, he would, very possibly, have done much good for the cause of Christ. But would he have been able to open up the Church to the whole world of the gentiles so successfully? We have only to read his words in Acts 11 and Acts 15 to appreciate this. The time he seemingly "wasted" in dealing with God and discovering his will was time that gave rich dividends indeed.

I think with envy of those men of Acts who were so completely under the influence of the Holy Spirit in all their apostolic work. Philip the evangelist is sent by the Spirit to the desert road of Gaza. Who in the world would think of going to that desert strip of land as a place that would yield apostolic results? No amount of planning or position papers or statistics or sociological surveys would have shown this to Philip. Only the Spirit can give us such seemingly foolish directions if our ears are unclogged with the noise of the world and of our selfish desires.

Or take that marvelous passage of Acts 16 that must arouse the envy of any apostle who is struggling to find God's will.

They travelled through the Phrygian and Galatian region, because they were prevented by the Holy Spirit from delivering the message in the province of Asia; and when they approached the Mysian border they tried to enter Bithynia; but the Spirit of Jesus would not allow them, so they skirted Mysia and reached the coast at Troas. During the night a vision came to Paul: a Macedonian stood there appealing to him and saying, "Come across to Macedonia and help us." After he had seen this vision we at once set about getting a passage to Macedonia, concluding that God had called us to bring them the good news.

Acts 16:6–10

Paul was certainly in constant touch with headquarters. We know from 2 Corinthians 12 that he was a contemplative, an outstanding mystic. But prayer was certainly no escape for him. It was reporting for orders on where to go, how long to stay there, what to do, what to say. It was living, loving intercourse with the Risen Lord that not only gave Paul the guidance he needed but also brought him encouragement and fortitude. After his conversion, he is praying in the temple of Jerusalem when he falls into a trance and, in his own words,

I saw him there, speaking to me. "Make haste," he said, "and leave Jerusalem without delay, for they will not accept your testimony about me." "Lord," I said, "they know that I imprisoned those who believe in thee, and flogged them in every synagogue; and when the blood of Stephen thy witness was shed I stood by, approving, and I looked after the clothes of those who killed him." But he said to me, "Go, for I am sending you far away to the Gentiles."

Acts 22:17–22

When he is in Corinth the going becomes tough; the Risen Lord appears again to encourage his ambassador.

One night in a vision the Lord said to Paul, "Have no fear: go on with your preaching and do not be silenced, for I am with you and no one shall attempt to do you harm; and there are many in this city who are my people."

Acts 18:9–11

Similarly, during his final arrest, the Lord himself comes to commend him and tell him where he will go next:

The following night the Lord appeared to him and said, "Keep up your courage; you have affirmed the truth about me in Jerusalem, and you must do the same in Rome."

Acts 23:11

How to Acquire These Characteristics of an Apostle

There was nothing we could do to acquire or merit our vocation to the apostolate. This was a pure gift of the Lord. Similarly, there is nothing we can do to merit or acquire the things that most characterize the apostle: the encounter with Christ, the ability to impart the Spirit, the discernment of God's will. These too, are pure gifts. Well, there is something we can do to get these gifts from the Lord. We can (a) desire them ardently and (b) ask for them constantly.

Christ generally appears, the Holy Spirit is generally given, to people of great desires. The day a burning desire for God arises within your heart, rejoice, because it won't be long before the desire is fulfilled. Unfortunately, however, there are many who don't even have this desire. They have lost their appetite for God. If this is true of you, don't be discouraged. Do you at least want this appetite for God? Yes? Then all is well! You must then fall back on the second means of the two I mentioned above: you must make diligent use of petitionary prayer: pray for the grace to meet Christ (this is your right and privilege as an apostle); pray to receive the outpouring of the Spirit; pray to recover your appetite for God. Surely, this is nothing very difficult that is being asked of you. Just sit like a beggar in the presence of the Lord tomorrow and keep rattling your begging bowl until he fills it. Refuse to take "No" or "Later" for an answer. The Lord loves this kind of loving persistence, chiefly when the gift we are insisting on receiving is the gift of himself. Be like the Canaanite woman of Matthew 15 who refused to be put off even by a clear rebuff of the Lord—and how the Lord loved and admired her for it! Or be like the centurion of Mathew 9: "One word of yours, Lord, is enough—all you have to do is say one single word." How warmly the Lord responded to that kind of prayer too!

So make this sort of prayer tomorrow! Take an ejaculation and repeat it ceaselessly: "Lord, teach me to pray" or "Lord, I want you with all my heart." Or borrow the words of the psalmist, "My soul is thirsting for you"; "As the deer longs for streams of living water, so do I long for you."

You may feel tired or bored after a while. But persist in prayer. No single word of petition you say is really wasted. The Lord hears every single word of supplication that comes from your lips. If he delays a while in coming, in order to strengthen your faith, he certainly won't delay too long. And you will have the thrilling experience of discovering the immense power there is in prayer, if you haven't discovered it already.

There's something else you can do, particularly if you feel you are something of a "desperate case." You can get Our Lady to put in a word for you. See what she was able to achieve at the wedding feast of Cana! If you do this, you will make another thrilling discovery (if you haven't made it yet) that Mary's influence with Christ is enormous and that the apostle has in her intercession a source of enormous strength and comfort and peace.

3

Dispositions for Starting a Retreat

Why Make a Retreat?

Each one of you has come to this retreat with some expectations. It is a great help to make these expectations explicit. I have sometimes participated in Encounter Groups where the first thing the participants are invited to do is to express their expectations and fears: What is it you fear in this Encounter? Imagine yourself leaving this group after the sessions are over; what would you like to have gained from it? In other words, what do you expect, concretely, from this Encounter? This helps greatly to clarify goals and to draw more profit from the experience of the Encounter Group.

This is what I invite you to do in prayer, either tonight before you go to bed, or tomorrow in your morning prayer. Ask yourself: Do I have any fears about making this retreat? What are they? Do I bring any expectations to this retreat? What are they, concretely?

People come with very varied expectations, some will want to deepen their prayer life; others to overcome some defect or rid themselves of some inordinate attachment or fear; yet others to find out God's will for themselves. Once you have faced your fears and concretized your expectations you may want to talk them over with your spiritual director, and discuss what you ought to do to achieve your goals during these precious retreat days.

One very legitimate expectation that people have of the type of retreat I am offering you is this: they expect to experience God, to encounter him more deeply, more powerfully. This is a retreat, not a seminar. So it is geared to giving you not theology, not even "spirituality," but an experience: the experience of God, the experience of falling in love with him and the experience of being deeply loved by him. This sort of experience will effect in your heart what no amount of theology or learning will, good and useful as these are in their proper place and time.

We who claim to be apostles are particularly in need of this experience in our lives if we are going to offer to others, not just formulas about God, but God himself. How will you ever introduce others to a God or a Jesus Christ whom you yourself have never met? You surely know that the world today is sick of words. The market is glutted with books and more books and still more books; with ideas, ideas, ideas; with talk, talk, talk. What the world is looking for is *action* and *experience*. It won't be patient with God-talk any longer. The modern world is saying, Show me; where is this God of yours? Can I meet him in my life? If not, of what use is he to me? If so, how? Where? The modern world is becoming increasingly atheist. What proof is there that there is a God? One Hindu book puts it so well. "The finest proof of his existence," it says, "is union with him." If we can offer to others the experience of union with God and the peace and joy that this experience brings, we will have much less difficulty bringing atheists to God.

The World's Hunger for God

Before Charles Davis left the priesthood, he wrote an article in *America* magazine that, in hindsight, is very poignant. He said something like this in that article:

After Vatican II I was enthusiastic about the prospects there were for Church renewal, for updating and changing struc-

tures. I would offer to packed audiences the wonderful new
theology of Vatican II that contained such rich potential for ag-
giornamento and reform. But gradually, it dawned upon me
that all those faces turned up toward me were not seeking a
new theology: they were seeking God. They were not looking
up to me as a theologian with a message, but as a priest, who
might be able to offer them God. They were obviously hungry
for God. Then I would look into myself and realize, with a
sinking heart that I could not offer them God; I barely had him
myself! There was a great void in my heart—and the busier I
was with things like Church reform and updating structures,
even with the liturgical renewal and scripture studies and pastoral methods, the easier it was for me to escape from God, to
escape from the void in my heart.

That, more or less, is the gist of what Charles Davis had to say
in that article. How many of us priests have to admit as true of ourselves what he frankly confessed about himself? If the priest comes
to the modern world equipped with every conceivable talent but
lacks the direct, personal experience of God, the world will simply
refuse to take his God-talk seriously and will have little use for him
as priest, much as it may value him as an educator or philosopher
or scientist.

What the modern world, and in particular the younger generation, is saying to us today—"Don't just talk, show me"—is what
India has been saying to us for centuries. I remember good Father
Abhishiktananda telling me, some years ago, of a holy Hindu he
met in the South of India, who said to him, "You missionaries will
never have any impact on us unless you come to us as gurus." The
guru is a man who doesn't merely talk about what he has read in a
book. He talks from the assurance of his own religious experience.
He guides his disciples with a sure touch because he leads them
along paths to God that he has himself traversed, not just read
about. It will profit us little to tell our Hindu brothers and sisters

about the experience of a man called John of the Cross whose works we have in our libraries and of whom we are justifiably proud. They will be interested, but not impressed. They will say, "That's fine. And what has your experience of God been? You come to us with theology and liturgy and scripture and canon law. But behind all these rites and words and concepts is a Reality that these rites symbolize and these concepts cover inadequately. Are you in direct touch with this Reality? Can you put me in touch with It?"

Some Suggestions

If the experience of God is one of your expectations, then a retreat like this one is just the thing for you. I shall offer you a number of suggestions during these days to help you dispose yourself to experience God, to pray and communicate with him in greater depth. There are some suggestions I should like to make right now.

1. Observe silence strictly all through the day.

A few years ago it was self-evident that the voice of God is heard best in silence; that a retreat should be made in silence. This is no longer obvious to many people. Silence is a discipline on the ear more than on the tongue. We silence our tongues in order that we may hear better. How hard it is to pick up subtle sounds when we are talking! And the voice of God is a very delicate, subtle sound, particularly for ears that are not accustomed to it. If your ears are not accustomed to hearing God's voice then you are in special need of silence. A conductor will detect the sound of a fragile instrument like a flute even in the midst of the crashing sounds of a hundred instruments in the orchestra. The untrained ear needs to be exposed to that flute alone for quite some time before it can recognize it unerringly in the midst of the orchestra. And we need to be exposed to God's voice in silence for a long time if we are later to detect it amidst the noise of the marketplace.

Modern humanity finds silence particularly irksome. We find it hard to sit still with ourselves. We are always itching to be up and about, to do something, to say something; we cannot act, and so most of our activity is not free, creative, dynamic as we like to think it is; it is compulsive. When you acquire the ability to sit still and be silent, you will be *free* to act or not, to speak or not, and then your speech and your activity will take on new depth and power.

Modern humanity is suffering a serious crisis of superficiality. We can't go deep into ourselves because the moment we attempt to do this we are cast out of our own heart as the sea casts out a dead body. One author has put it eloquently: human beings cannot be happy unless they get in touch with the springs of life in the depths of their souls; however, they are constantly exiled from their own home, locked out of their own spiritual solitude; so they cease to be a person. The poet Kahlil Gibran says, "You talk when you are no longer at peace with yourself. And when you can no longer dwell in the depths of your heart, you live on your lips. And sound becomes a diversion and a pastime."

Do you want a simple test of how much you yourself are a victim of the crisis of superficiality? See if you are comfortable with silence. How much silence can you endure without the compulsion to talk? This is far from being the only criterion of depth, but it is a fairly good one.

2. Avoid reading.

Keep away from all reading except Scripture and books that clearly foster prayer, books like *The Imitation of Christ*. A book may help prayer, but during a retreat it frequently becomes a hindrance to facing God. You can bury your head in a book the way a man buries his head in a newspaper when he is avoiding contact with people. When the going gets tough and communication with God becomes frustrating and dry (as sooner or later it is bound to become) the temptation to take refuge in a book is very strong. Then, instead of exposing yourself with courage to the rigors and frustrations of making contact with God, instead of enduring the pain of dryness and desolation, you will anesthetize yourself with an interesting book. Learn to battle against your distractions, to bear your coldness of heart patiently without crutches like books; the pain will be purifying. This is one of the standard trials of the contemplative life. Your prayer will deepen if you bear the trial and the pain, not shield yourself against it with a book.

Not only in time of prayer, but at other times too during the retreat, stay away from books, just as you stay away from conversation with others. Be silent and attentive to God all through the day, not just in time of prayer and do not give in to the distraction of reading—a pious distraction, no doubt, but a distraction nonetheless.

For many people spiritual reading, while very valuable, even necessary, in their *spiritual life*, is no help at all in *time of prayer*. It is a kind of drug with which to ease the pains of contemplation. I must add, however that for some people taking small doses of this drug would be better than total abstention. If after a couple of bookless days you suspect that this is true of you, I invite you to talk the matter over with your spiritual director. Most retreatants say to me after a couple of days, "Reading? But there's just no time to read." That's generally a good sign that they have really taken off the ground.

3. Invest time heavily in prayer.

Give all the time you can to prolonged hours of silent dealing with God. This is the way to get the maximum profit from the retreat. It is the toughest way, but decidedly the best. If you invest much time, your prayer life will improve considerably and this will be a lasting treasure you will take with you from this retreat.

Most retreatants give from five to six hours a day to prayer, not counting the time given to the Eucharist, the Office, and shared prayer at night. That isn't too much at all; I once made a retreat under a Buddhist. He had us wake up at four in the morning and meditate for an average of twelve hours a day. Some of our number put in as many as fourteen or fifteen hours. That's intensity for you. I thought amusedly of our Catholic retreats where people generally think they have done something heroic by praying for six hours a day.

I'll have more to say later about giving time to prayer. Here I shall content myself with advising you to pray much and to have fixed periods of prayer of an hour or more each time. I insist on the "fixed period"; set a time when you begin and when you end. This is a great help to most people who would otherwise "pray all through the day," but whose prayer would lack depth and intensity because it is too general and vague. So fix your times for prayer, and pray outside these times too, of course.

The Desire for God

If you wish to attain a deeper experience of God in this retreat, you must bring two vital dispositions with you. If you do not have these dispositions, you must give time at the beginning of the retreat to acquiring them. The first of these dispositions is a desire for God; the second is courage and generosity.

The desire for God: God cannot resist the one who desires him ardently. I was much impressed by the Hindu story of a villager who came to a sannyasi (a holy man) while he was meditating under a tree and said to him, "I want to see God. Show me how I can experience God." The sannyasi, typically, said nothing. He continued with his meditation. The good villager returned with the same request next day—and the next and next and next, though he received no reply until, seeing his perseverance, the sannyasi at last said to him, "You seem to be a genuine seeker after God. This afternoon I shall go down to the river for my bath. Meet me there." When the two of them were in the water the sannyasi grasped the head of the man firmly, pushed it under the water and held it there for a couple of minutes while the poor man struggled to come out of the water. After a couple of minutes the sannyasi released him and said, "Come again to the banyan tree tomorrow." When he came the next day it was the sannyasi who spoke first. "Tell me," he said, "why did you struggle so much while I held your head under the water?" "Because," said the man, "I was gasping for air—without air I would have died." Then the sannyasi smiled and said, "The day you desire God as desperately as you desired air, you will surely find him."

That is the chief reason why we do not find God: we do not desire him ardently enough. Our lives are crowded with far too many other things and we can get on pretty well without God. He is certainly not as essential to us as the air we breathe. This is what he was to a man like Ramakrishna. Each time I think of his life I feel deeply moved. He was barely sixteen years old and already a priest in a Hindu temple, charged with performing the rites of the temple deity. He was seized with a longing to penetrate through the veil of the temple idol and get in touch with the Infinite Reality that the idol symbolized, a Reality he called "Mother." This became such an obsession with him that he would sometimes forget to perform the rites. At other times, he would begin waving the sacred lamp before the deity and, seized with his obsession, would absentmindedly continue to wave it for hours until someone would come in and bring him to his senses and stop him. He had all the signs of a man who was deeply, passionately in love. Each night before retiring to sleep he would sit before the deity and cry, "Mother, another day has passed and I have still not found you! How long must I wait, Mother, how long?" And he would weep bitterly. How can God resist such longings? Is it any wonder that Ramakrishna became the extraordinary mystic he was? He once said to a friend, speaking about what it means to long for God, "If a thief were sleeping in a room that was separated from a treasury full of gold only by a thin wall, would he sleep? All night long he would be awake contriving devices to get at that gold. When I was a youngster, I desired God even more ardently than that thief desired gold."

St. Augustine tells us of the great restlessness of the human heart that cannot rest till it has found its rest in God. Without God, for whom we are created, we are like fish out of water. If we do not experience the agony of the fish it is only because we kill the pain with a host of other desires and pleasures, even problems, which we allow to occupy our minds and which we allow to suppress the desire for God and the pain of not having him yet.

If you do not have this kind of desire for God, ask for it. It is a grace that the Lord gives to all whom he wishes to reveal himself to. Hopefully the retreat, by quieting the other cravings in your heart, will bring this deep-rooted desire to the surface.

Generosity and Courage

This is the second disposition you need. To pray is no easy task, particularly when you invest a long time in prayer. You will experience strong resistances within you—feelings of boredom, of disgust, even of fear as your prayer becomes deeper. No less a person than St. Teresa of Avila says there were times when she would feel so disgusted with prayer that she had to summon up all her courage to make herself even enter her oratory. "I know how grievous such trials are," she says. "They need more courage than do many trials in the world." And no one can accuse St. Teresa of not knowing what trials in the world are—she was very much out there in the world, battling to establish her Carmelite reformed convents throughout Spain. So, to persevere in prayer these days you are going to need generosity with God, and courage.

There's another reason why you need courage and generosity: it isn't just that prayer itself can be a demanding exercise but that the God you meet in prayer is going to lay bare your rationalizations, to break down your defenses, to make you see yourself as you really are—and this can be very painful. The encounter with God is not always a pleasant, soothing experience. Someone has said rightly that the encounter is surgical before it becomes soothing. The God of the Bible is encountered in a command. Each time someone experiences him in the Bible it is in connection with some sacrifice that has to be made, something that must be given up, some task that has to be undertaken, generally an unpleasant task. Witness the reluctance of people like Jeremiah and Moses to accept the unpleasant task God lays on their shoulders. If you want to meet God you must be ready to hear his voice calling you to something you may not like.

> When you were young you fastened your belt about you and walked where you chose; but when you are old you will stretch out your arms, and a stranger will bind you fast, and carry you where you have no wish to go.
>
> John 21:18

This does not mean that we must be fearful. The words we hear will not just be demanding words. They will be loving words, strengthening words. God will give us the love and strength we need to measure up to his demands. But we cannot gloss over the fact that the demands are there, that he is calling us to die to ourselves. And death is something that frightens us initially.

You must approach God with no conditions, in a state of complete self-surrender. If you start out by saying, "Ask me for anything except this" or "Command anything except such and such," you are putting a serious obstacle in the way of your encountering God. I am *not* saying you are expected to have the strength to do what God wants you to do. Quite the contrary: you are expected *not* to have the strength, poor, weak creature that you are. Strength is something that comes from God, not from ourselves. It is his business to provide it.

What is expected of us is honesty—that we do not deceive

ourselves, that we face the truth about ourselves, our cowardice, our selfishness, our possessiveness, and shed our rationalizations. The moment we get into prayer, we shall notice voices coming up within us that we would rather not hear. What is demanded of us is the courage to listen, and not block our ears, not look the other way, no matter how unpleasant this might be.

Do not start out with the prejudice that God simply could not be asking this or that of you, that such and such would be silly or stupid. God has no inhibitions whatsoever about demanding the foolish and stupid thing of us. What could be more foolish than that salvation should come through the Cross? What more ridiculous than that the apostles should speak in tongues and expose themselves to the charge of being drunk? Indeed our overpowering desire to be always rational and balanced and respectable is one of the major obstacles to holiness. We want to appear proper and well balanced, to do what is reasonable and respectable and conventional; in other words, what society considers proper and reasonable. The Holy Spirit can be downright "unreasonable" by worldly standards, and the saints, by these same standards, were mad. Indeed, the dividing line between holiness and madness is a very thin one; it is frequently hard to distinguish one from the other. If we would be great saints and do great things for God we must lose our fear of being considered crazy; we must lose concern for our good name. So let us not exclude "crazy" things from the list of things God could be demanding of us. Let us approach him with minds and hearts open to anything he wants, no matter how crazy or difficult it seems at first sight.

Gospel Texts

Here are some texts that may help you with your prayer tomorrow morning:

Matthew 13:44–46: The parable of the pearl merchant and the parable of the hidden treasure. Here are crazy men for you. Imagine a man stumbling upon that precious pearl at a jeweler's shop. His heart skips a beat! Here is an extraordinary jewel indeed. This man knows a good stone when he sees one. What is the price? 10,000 rupees. 10,000 rupees? Even to think of a sum as great as that is crazy, for he isn't a rich man. So he goes away—but the thought of that pearl just won't leave him. He is obsessed with it. Then a truly crazy scheme takes shape in his mind: suppose he were to sell his house, his land, his tools of labor his very clothes—just everything (Jesus explicitly says he sold everything he had). If into this sum he threw all his savings, he would just be able to scrape together those 10,000 rupees. How much doubt he must have gone through before he took that vital decision! Is it worth risking everything, indeed, actually losing everything for the sake of one pearl? What will the neighbors say? But when you are obsessed with something, all other considerations fall by the wayside. The fool actually sold everything and got his pearl. That is the type of man who gets God—the man who gives everything, the man whom everyone laughs at and considers a fool. But Jesus tells us that this kind of man goes away *joyfully*. Great mystery! He has lost everything—and he is filled with joy. Here is the pearl, the pearl of joy, of peace, that God gives to those who give up everything for his sake. But mind you, it must be *everything*. God deals in fixed prices: 9,000 rupees won't buy you that joy, nor 9,900, not even 9,999—give everything and you will receive everything. By contrast we have the rich young man of Matthew 19—he has vast possessions and he goes away *sad!* True and lasting joy is found only in total renunciation.

We have a living model of this in Paul who in Philippians 3:7–22 says so movingly of himself that he did indeed lose everything for Christ:

> But all such assets I have written off because of Christ. I would say more: I count everything sheer loss, because all is far outweighed by the gain of knowing Christ Jesus my Lord, for

whose sake I did in fact lose everything. I count it so much garbage, for the sake of gaining Christ and finding myself incorporate in him. . . . All I care for is to know Christ, to experience the power of his resurrection, and to share his sufferings, in growing conformity with his death, if only I may finally arrive at the resurrection from the dead.

"All I want is to know Christ." Can we say those words of ourselves? Is it true that this is *all* we desire? If it is so, then we have already found God or are certainly on the verge of finding him.

You may want to take Luke 14:26ff. or Matthew 10:37–39 and consider the words of Jesus there as addressed to you. You may find inspiration in Genesis 12, where Abraham becomes a wanderer in obedience to God or Genesis 22 where he is asked to sacrifice his son Isaac. There is also Luke 9:57–10:9 and the inspiring cry of Paul that nothing can separate him from the love of Christ, in Romans 8:35.

Or you may find these texts too demanding, too frightening for your weakness. Then take Acts 1:4–5, 8, 11 where you see the apostles praying for the Spirit who will take away their cowardice and give them the courage they are going to need for the apostolate. Do what they themselves did: (a) Don't leave Jerusalem—stay in your solitude and cut yourself away from all unnecessary intercourse with others. (b) Wait patiently for a power which you will "receive"—it cannot be produced by any efforts of your own. (c) Pray persistently together with Mary and the saints. Or take Luke 11:1–13. It will encourage you to ask for the Holy Spirit with confidence.

Or, finally, take 1 Timothy 1:15–17 where you will find those encouraging words of Paul: "God has done marvellous things through me, great sinner that I am, so that he might make an example of me to others, for if he could work wonders with a man like me, what will he not do for others who trust in him."

Whatever you do, whatever texts you take for prayer, for

heaven's sake don't seek to *produce* what is actually a pure gift of God: the courage and generosity you are seeking is so heroic, the desire for God you need is so intense that no human being can produce it within his own heart. This is a gift of God, a gift that is *always* given to humble, persistent petitionary prayer. So pray for courage. Pray for power. Pray for honesty. Pray for these gifts, not just for yourself, but for all of us who are making this retreat. Pray that we shall all experience a new Pentecost during these days. That each single person here will receive the Holy Spirit abundantly and experience his transforming power in his or her life.

4

How to Pray

I want to talk to you tonight about something you have come to this retreat to do. You have come here to pray. So I want to speak about prayer, what it is and how to make it. However, before entering into this topic let me say something to you about two related topics. The first is the need of the experience of God for an apostle, the second, silence.

The Apostle's Need for an Experience of God

Swami Vivekananda tells somewhere of his first encounter with Ramakrishna. The incident illustrates very well what I want to say on this point. Vivekananda, whose name was then Narendra, was a precocious, somewhat conceited young college student who claimed he was an agnostic. He had heard about the holiness of Ramakrishna, so he went to visit him. He found him squatting on his bed. The conversation went something like this:

Narendra: Do you believe in God, Sir?
Ramakrishna: Yes, I do.
Narendra: Well, I don't. What is it that makes you believe
    in him? Can you prove to me he exists, Sir?
Ramakrishna: Yes.

Narendra: Why are you so sure you will be able to convince me?

Ramakrishna: Because at this moment I see him more clearly than I see you.

The tone of voice in which those words were said, and the expression on Ramakrishna's face overwhelmed Narendra. He was never the same again. Those words changed him completely. That is the way it is with the words, and indeed, the whole being of someone who is in direct touch with God. It is disturbing to be in the presence of those who truthfully make the claim that they can sense God and see him—someone like Moses of whom Scripture says, "He was resolute, as one who saw the invisible God" (Hebrews 11:27).

This is the whole point of our being apostles. The apostle is not just someone with a message. Apostles are their message. When we point out the way of holiness, people will not look at the direction our finger is pointing in. The first thing they will look at is *us*. This is our greatest apostolic need today—not better planning, better equipment, better surveys, better knowledge of our people, their language, their customs, better conversion techniques (if such things exist at all!) but better human beings; a whole new breed of human beings whose lives are evidently charged with the power and presence of the Holy Spirit.

The Identity Crisis

So many priests and religious are undergoing today what is known as an identity crisis. The priest no longer knows what he is and what he is supposed to be in the modern world. This constitutes a problem, yes. But a crisis? We have, no doubt, to study and reflect so as to come up with a more adequate theological definition of what a priest really is, and I can see the liberating effect this will have for the life and work of many priests. But does this lack of an adequate theological definition have to constitute a *crisis* for a priest?

Is a happily married layperson in a state of personal crisis because we are still in search of an adequate theological definition of marriage (and, for that matter, always shall be, given the richness of different cultures and of spiritual realities and the limitations of the human mind)? True, a better definition and a better understanding of marriage will be a help to our laypersons in their married lives. But in the meantime they are experiencing the reality of marriage even though they are not in possession of its definition. They love their spouses and children and are loved by them; they experience the growth and fulfillment which the joys and pains of married life bring with them. There is no reason to be in a state of crisis.

The Imitation of Christ is very wise when it says, "I had rather experience compunction than be able to define it." May we not say the same of many modern priests who are undergoing their identity crisis? Have they *experienced* the meaning of their priesthood and not just *talked* about it? Are they in love with Christ? Are they full of the Spirit? Do they have the fulfillment that comes from giving the Spirit to others, from bringing Christ into the lives of others? If they have, I don't see how they can be going through an identity crisis any more than the happily married people I spoke of earlier. But in order to experience love for Christ you must first have met Christ. In order to give the Holy Spirit you must have experienced his power in your own life. This is what the retreat is all about. It is not a seminar where we speak about Christ. It is a period of silence when we speak to Christ. The speaking about will come later. Let us meet him first, develop an intimacy with him. Then we will truly have something to talk about.

Silence

This brings me to my second topic. There are few things that help so much for conversing with Christ as silence. The silence I speak of is, obviously, the inner silence of the heart without which the voice of Christ will simply not be heard. This inner silence is very hard to achieve for most of us: close your eyes for a moment and observe what is going on within you. The chances are you will be submerged in a sea of thoughts that you are powerless to stop— talk, talk, talk (for that is what thinking generally is, me talking to myself)—noise, noise, noise: my own inner voice competing with the remembered voices and images of others, all clamoring for my attention. What chances does the subtle voice of God stand in all this din and bustle?

Exterior silence is an enormous help for attaining interior silence. If you cannot bear to observe exterior silence, if, in other words, it is unbearable for you to keep your mouth shut, how will you bear the silence that is interior? How will you keep your inner mouth shut? Your tolerance of silence is a fairly good indicator of your spiritual (and even intellectual and emotional) depth. It is possible that when you shut your mouth the noise inside you will become even louder, your distractions will increase, you will be even less able to pray. This is not caused by silence. The noise was there all along. Silence is only making you aware of it and giving you the opportunity to quiet and master it.

Jesus tells us to shut the door when we go to pray. We are obviously not shutting the rest of the world out of our hearts, for we will take its concerns with us to prayer. But that door must be firmly shut or else the noisy world will come in and drown out the voice of God, chiefly in the early stages when concentration does not come easily to us. And the beginner in prayer needs no less concentration than the beginner in mathematics who cannot work on a complex problem when there is a lot of distracting noise around him. The time will come when students of prayer, like mathematics students, will be so gripped by their subject that no amount of noise will be able to take their minds away from their subject. But in the early stages let them be humble and admit their need for quiet and for silence.

The Saints on Silence

The saints have spoken eloquently of the value of silence. Here are a couple of quotes I picked up from a book of Thomas Merton. One is from a Syrian monk, Isaac of Nineveh. What he says is as true for the solitary in the desert as for the apostle in the heart of a modern city. He says,

> Many are continually seeking, but they alone find who remain in continual silence. . . . Every man who delights in a multitude of words, even though he says admirable things, is empty within. If you love truth, be a lover of silence. Silence like the sunlight will illuminate you in God and will deliver you from the phantoms of ignorance. Silence will unite you to God himself. . . . More than all things, love silence: it brings you a fruit that tongue cannot describe. In the beginning, we have to force ourselves to be silent. But then there is born something that draws us to silence. May God give you an experience of this "something" that is born of silence. If only you practise this, untold light will dawn on you in consequence . . . after a while a certain sweetness is born in the heart of this exercise and the body is drawn almost by force to remain in silence.

Every word in those lines is worth meditating on. These words will speak powerfully to the heart of anyone who has ever experienced the treasures there are in silence.

The other quote on silence is from a desert Father, Ammonas, a disciple of St. Anthony:

> Behold, my beloved, I have shown you the power of silence, how thoroughly it heals and how fully pleasing it is to God. Wherefore I have written to you to show yourselves strong in this work you have undertaken, so that you may know that it

is by silence that the power of God dwelt in them, because of silence that the mysteries of God were known to them.

Isaac of Nineveh is obviously speaking from experience when he says, "In the beginning we have to *force* ourselves to be silent." Silence doesn't come easily to us at the start. When we try to observe it we shall notice strong resistances within us: Eveyln Underhill tells us the value of overcoming these resistances in her book *Mysticism:*

> The self is as yet unacquainted with the strange plane of silence which so soon becomes familiar to those who attempt even the lowest activities of the contemplative live; where the self is released from succession, the voices of the world are never heard and the great adventures of the spirit take place.

Adventures, indeed. You will make thrilling discoveries once you have suffered through the initial boredom and restlessness that silence brings. You will find that this dark silence is really filled with heavenly light and with heavenly music; that what at first sight seemed empty and nothingness is really filled with the presence of God. A presence that it is impossible to describe but that is somehow conveyed so attractively in the words of Simone Weil, when she tries to describe the effects she felt on reciting the Lord's Prayer:

> At times the very first words tear my thoughts from my body and transport it to a place outside space where there is neither perspective nor point of view. . . . At the same time, filling every part of this infinity of infinity, there is a silence, a silence which is not an absence of sound but which is the object of a positive sensation, more positive than that of sound. Noises, if there are any, only reach me after crossing the silence.

After listening to these words, I imagine that you need no further urgings from me to plunge into strict silence these days—for you are not likely to get such a fine opportunity in the rest of the year and the effects of silence are cumulative, that is, the silence that comes after four days of silence is deeper than the silence you have at the start of the retreat.

How to Pray:
Jesus the Master of Prayer

If this retreat is to give you the rich fruit you are expecting of it you must invest a long time in prayer. And if you are to pray well you must know how to pray. How are you to pray? This is a question that the apostles asked of Jesus. And Jesus himself taught them what they were to do when they were in prayer. This is fortunate for us, because we too can learn from him how to pray. There is no better master in the art of prayer; in fact, for us Christians, there is no other master.

In Luke 11 we read, "Once, in a certain place, Jesus was at prayer. When he ceased, one of his disciples said 'Lord, teach us to pray, as John taught his disciples.'" How wise of the apostles to have direct recourse to the Master when they wanted to learn how to pray. I advise you to do the same. No one can teach you to pray, really. I certainly cannot. The conferences I shall be giving you these days will, please God, be something of a help to you in your prayer life. But, sooner or later, you are going to run into difficulties that no earthly teacher will be able to solve for you, and you will have to have direct recourse to Jesus and say to him, "Lord, teach me to pray." And he will solve your difficulties for you and guide you personally. So I advise you, right from the start, whenever you run into difficulties and find the going tough, to look at Jesus and say, "Lord, teach me to pray." Say it again and again—for the whole day if need be. Say it without strain or anxiety, calmly, in the firm expectation that he will teach you; as indeed he will! Here then is the first answer to the question, "How to pray?" Go to Jesus and ask him to teach you. That is how you learn to pray.

God-Centered Prayer

Let us continue with that gospel passage and see what kind of teaching the Lord gives on prayer. "He answered, 'When you pray, say, Father, thy name be hallowed; thy kingdom come.' " Here's something about the type of prayer that Jesus teaches. He teaches us to begin not with ourselves but with the Father; not with our interests and needs but with his kingdom. "Set your mind on God's kingdom and his justice before everything else, and all the rest will come to you as well" (Matthew 6:33). Jesus' prayer was essentially God-centered, as was his whole life. We speak of him today as the man for others, as indeed he was. But he was even more the man for his Father. The Gospels make it abundantly clear that the one great obsession in Jesus' life was not humankind, but his Father. His food and drink was to do the will of his Father. We would be his brothers and sisters and mother only if we did the will of his Father. He is less concerned with our calling him, "Lord, Lord," than with doing his Father's will as he himself did. In fact, he is clearly obsessed with trying to get all of us to be lovers and worshipers of the Father as he himself was. We like to think that it was out of love for us that he went to his passion, and so it was. However, it is sobering to realize that, for all the love he had for us, he recoiled from the passion; he did not want it; the only thing that made him go through it was his Father. Father, take this cup away from me; I do not want it; but if you want it for me I shall take it. "So that the world may know that I love the Father, and do exactly as he commands, up, let us go forward!" (John 14:31).

Here then is the first lesson that Jesus gives us when he teaches us to pray. He teaches us to begin with God; to be concerned about the coming of his kingdom, about his name being glorified, about his holy will being done everywhere. This is one of the reasons why our prayer fails: it is too self-centered, too human-centered. We must get out of ourselves and center ourselves on God and his kingdom.

Jesus will make us pray for ourselves too. None of that superior kind of holy indifference that says, I'm just not bothered about myself—I leave all my needs to God. No, sir! Jesus will have none of this. We must become humble, accept the fact that we have needs, even material needs, and beg God to fulfill these needs. Jesus bids us ask for three things for ourselves: for our daily bread (for bread, not luxuries!), for spiritual strength, and for forgiveness of sin.

Petitionary Prayer

Have you noticed something in the prayer Jesus teaches his apostles? From start to finish it is petitionary prayer: "Father, may your name be glorified, may your kingdom come, may your will be done . . ." Even these things are the subject of our petition! The kingdom of God is going to come even more surely than the sun is going to rise. And yet Jesus bids us ask that it may come.

This is what prayer was for Jesus. Prayer, as he taught it to the apostles, meant asking for things we need, asking for what is good for us. As if to confirm this Jesus gives us a kind of commentary on the Our Father. He says,

> Suppose one of you has a friend who comes to him in the middle of the night and says, My friend, lend me three loaves, for a friend of mine on a journey has turned up at my house, and I have nothing to offer him: and he replies from inside, do not bother me. The door is shut for the night; my children and I have gone to bed; and I cannot get up and give you what you want. I tell you that even if he will not provide for him out of friendship, the very shamelessness of the request will make him get up and give him all he needs. And so I say to you, ask and you will receive; seek and you will find; knock, and the door will be opened. For everyone who asks receives, he who seeks finds, and to him who knocks, the door will be opened.

The words are positively startling in their simplicity: *everyone*—
no distinction between saints and sinners, no "ifs" or "buts"; *everyone* who asks will receive. It is as if this is too much to believe.
"These are hard words, and who can believe them?" All sorts of
doubts and reservations come to our minds. We have asked for
things so often and haven't received them; Jesus could hardly mean
literally what he says. So he rubs it in, so to speak.

> Is there a father among you who will offer his son a snake when
> he asks for fish, or a scorpion when he asks for an egg? If you,
> then, bad as you are, know how to give your children what is
> good for them, how much more will the heavenly Father give
> the Holy Spirit to those who ask him!

This is a constant teaching of the New Testament: prayer is
powerful, prayer gives us all we need. And prayer is, basically, petitionary prayer. Here are some texts where you can check this for
yourself. I recommend that you read them prayerfully. They are
bound to strike you between the eyes—unless, of course, you have
known the power of petitionary prayer and been practicing it all
along. Matthew 21:20–22; Mark 11:22–26; Luke 11:1–13, 18:1, 8;
John 14:12–14, 15:7, 16:23–24; James 1:5–8, 5:13–18; 1 John 3:22,
5:14–15; Philippians 4:4–7; 1 Timothy 2:1ff.

The Key to the Art of Prayer

Somewhere early in my religious life I had the great good for-
tune of making a retreat under an extraordinary man, Father José
Calveras, who had the reputation of teaching people how to pray
during his retreats. I knew of venerable old Jesuits who had been
many years in religious life and came away from Father Calveras'
retreat saying, "This man has really taught me to pray"—not entirely accurate, of course, because there's barely any Christian who
doesn't know to pray in some way or other. I suppose what they

meant was that Calveras had taught them to pray more satisfactorily and in greater depth. This he certainly did for me.

I went to his retreat full of great expectations, but within a couple of days I was afflicted with all my usual prayer problems. When I took them to Father Calveras, he said to me, quite simply, "How do you pray?" (It struck me later that no one before had asked me that question point blank!) So I began to describe, step by step, what I did in prayer. "I take some point for meditation and get started on that," I said, "and within a minute or two my mind wanders. I'm hopelessly distracted." "What do you do then?" asked he. "Well, when I realize I am distracted (and that isn't too soon generally) I come back to the point I was meditating on." "And then?" said he. "Then I'm distracted again." "And then?" Calveras was very patient while I explained how, in my prayer, I moved from meditation to distraction, to meditation, to distraction—with the distraction generally accounting for ninety percent of the time. I have met dozens of people since then who have had exactly the same experience, and I wouldn't be surprised if this were the experience of most of you.

Father Calveras then said to me, "What you are doing is thinking—meditating. You are not *praying*. Nothing wrong with meditation, of course, provided it helps you to *pray*. Tell me, do you have your rosary with you?" (This, I should explain, was in the days before Vatican II—though I personally retain my devotion to the rosary even today.) "Yes," I said. "Pull it out, will you?" (I was a very young Jesuit and Calveras was an old man. He could do this sort of thing with impunity.) I did. "Do you know how to use that?" "Of course I do." "Then why don't you?" "What? You mean I should say the rosary during meditation?" I was a little shocked and showed it. What I did not show were the thoughts that went through my head; they were something like this: Does this man, this reputed master in the art of prayer, seriously expect me to say the rosary during meditation? I had come to associate the rosary with very simple, ignorant people—the prayer for farmers and fisherfolk, and the sort of thing you fell back upon if you were particularly disturbed in prayer and could do nothing else. A sort of second best. But I was perfectly capable of meditating—I had just completed my studies in philosophy!

Father Calveras in his quiet way went on, "Say a decade, praying to our Lady to obtain for you the grace of prayer, the grace to overcome your distractions. Then come back to your meditation if you wish. And if you are still distracted, say another decade and another. And, possibly, give up your meditation altogether and just pray for all the graces you need. Pray for your fellow retreatants. Pray for those you love. Pray for the world. The fruit of a retreat is not obtained through meditation and deep reflection. It is a pure gift of God and while a certain amount of reflection is helpful, even necessary, this gift is obtained through asking, through begging. So beg for it and the Lord will give it to you. Ask for the grace to pray. Ask for the grace to be generous with Christ. Ask for the grace of experiencing his love."

Father Calveras clearly took the gospel teaching on prayer quite literally. My later experience was to show me that this was the main reason why he was indeed a master in the art of prayer. He seriously believed, and taught us to believe, and all we had to do was to ask the Lord for what we needed, and the Lord would not let us down. He said to us, "The key to the art of prayer is the prayer of petition. Many people never learn to pray because they have never learned to make effective use of petitionary prayer. The hand outstretched to beg obtains what the hand pressed against one's head to think does not."

He said to me at that interview, "Do you like the Litany of the Saints? Or the Litany of our Lady? Yes? Then pray like this, slowly, attentively, 'Holy Mary, pray for me. Holy Mother of God, pray for me. Holy Virgin of Virgins, pray for me . . .' Can you pray like this?" Of course I could pray like that. The only trouble was that it seemed to me too easy. Surely, prayer must be something more complicated than this! I was later to read a book by Calveras in which he explained that simple vocal prayer and the devotional use of ejaculatory prayer is the antechamber to mysticism. I had been taught to look upon it as the prayer for beginners and the ignorant! To him, and indeed to anyone with some experience in the art of prayer, this was the prayer of the proficient.

Becoming a Child in Prayer

Father Calveras did indeed teach me to pray. From that day I've never been able to say honestly that I don't know how to pray. I've had my difficulties in prayer and, I'm sorry to say, I have not always been faithful to prayer. But I have never been able to say that I don't know how to pray. That simply wouldn't be true. I certainly do know how to pray. All I have to do is fall back on simple vocal prayer, on the prayer of petition. Any child can do this. That's the trouble with so many of us: we have ceased to be children, so we have forgotten how to pray.

Again and again, I have met priests and religious who prayed much better before they entered the novitiate or seminary than after. Does this surprise you? Many of you are probably in this category. Before we entered the novitiate, we prayed with such simplicity of heart. We had recourse to God, to the Blessed Virgin, in all our needs—for grace to pass our examinations, for health, for success in our work. Then we grew up and learned a lot of clever arguments about God not being interested in these mundane trifles. God helps those who help themselves, we cannot change the will of God, etc. So we stopped expecting miracles; we stopped praying for miracles; and God's interventions in our lives became fewer and fewer. In addition to this, we picked up complicated methods of prayer. We were taught how to reflect deeply; in other words, all the emphasis was given to reading and meditation and discursive prayer. We gradually became convinced that what we needed to become saints was deep convictions; and the way to deepen our convictions was to reflect, reflect, reflect; meditate, meditate, meditate. Whereas the truth of the matter is that what we need more than conviction, a thousand times more, if we are to be saints, is strength, spiritual power, courage, perseverance—and for this, we must ask, ask, ask; pray, pray, pray.

I shall deal with all these objections to petitionary prayer in another conference [conference 6—ed.]. For the time being it is sufficient that you expose yourselves to Christ's words on prayer in the Gospels. They will cause a wild hope to arise within your heart, even a certainty: if I pray earnestly for the Holy Spirit, I shall receive him—even today, this very day. Why not? You are very lucky indeed if God gives you this kind of faith, for then you will ask and you will surely receive. Mind you, I am *not* advising you to abandon meditation altogether. The very fact that I suggest you read those gospel passages, means I am inviting you to some form of meditation and reflection. What I am suggesting is that you stop placing your trust in meditation and start relying on the power of simple petitionary prayer and that you give this prayer much more importance than meditation. If you do this, you will discover the power that prayer brings, and the confidence and peace. You will realize the truth of Paul's words to the Philippians:

> The Lord is near: have no anxiety, but in everything make your requests known to God in prayer and petition with thanksgiving. Then the peace of God, which is beyond our utmost understanding, will keep guard over your hearts and your thoughts, in Christ Jesus.
>
> Philippians 4:6–7

And, having experienced the truth of these words for yourself, you will never abandon prayer for the rest of your life.

5

The Laws
of Prayer

Anyone who reads the words of Jesus on petitionary prayer with a fresh, unprejudiced mind, is bound to be impressed. Just ask, says Jesus, and you are bound to receive. A wild hope arises in our hearts. Can it really be true? Let me take him on faith and launch out, and I shall receive all I need and desire. But our experience frequently kills the hope. I have prayed so often in the past, and I have been disappointed so often. The words of Jesus couldn't possibly mean what they say. If they did, how can my frequent failure in prayer be explained?

The answer to that is simple enough. If you have not succeeded in prayer it is not because prayer does not work. It is because you have not learned to pray well. An engineer may complain that engineering doesn't work because every time he builds a bridge it collapses. The truth is that engineering works very well, but he is a bad engineer. If we fail in our prayer it is because we are bad prayers. We have failed to master the laws of prayer that Jesus clearly enunciated, for prayer has its own laws just as much as engineering.

The First Law of Prayer: Faith

Have you noticed the habit Jesus had of saying to anyone who came to him for a favor: Do you believe I can do this? In other words, he always insisted on faith in his power to heal and cure and work miracles. We are told that in his hometown, Nazareth, he could not work many miracles because of the lack of faith of the people there. It was almost a rigorous law with him: if you believe, all things are possible. If you do not believe, I can do nothing for you. You yourself need not have the faith: it is enough that someone else has it for you. (I shall later point this out as one of the advantages of shared prayer: you may ask the Lord for something, and your faith may be too weak for you to receive it; but the Lord will give you what you are asking for.) The daughter of Jairus had no faith; neither, as far as we know, did the servant of the centurion mentioned in Matthew 8:5, nor the paralytic of Matthew 9:2–8. It was enough that the petitioner, not necessarily the beneficiary, have faith. But faith there had to be. There was no substitute for it.

Jesus made a law out of this. In Matthew 21:18ff. we read:

Next morning on his way to the city he felt hungry; and seeing a fig-tree at the roadside he went up to it, but found nothing on it but leaves. He said to the tree, "You shall never bear fruit any more;" and the tree withered away at once. The disciples were amazed at the sight. "How is it," they asked, "that the tree withered so suddenly?" Jesus answered them, "I tell you this: if only you have faith and have no doubts, you will do what has been done to the fig-tree; and more than that, you need only say to this mountain, "Be lifted from your place and hurled into the sea," and what you say will be done. And whatever you pray for in faith you will receive.

Mark 11:20ff. says the same thing, more emphatically.

Early next morning, as they passed by, they saw that the fig-tree had withered from the roots up; and Peter, recalling what had happened, said to him, "Rabbi, look, the fig-tree which you cursed has withered." Jesus answered them, "Have faith in God. I tell you this: if anyone says to this mountain, 'Be lifted from your place and hurled into the sea,' and has no inward doubt but believes that what he says is happening, it will be done for him. I tell you, then, whatever you ask for in prayer, believe that you have received it and it will be yours."

This law of faith was well understood by the apostles, who handed it on to the early Christians. James puts it this way in his letter (1:5–8):

If any of you falls short of wisdom, he should ask God for it and it will be given him, for God is a generous giver who neither refuses nor reproaches anyone. But he must ask in faith, without a doubt in his mind; for the doubter is like a heaving sea ruffled by the wind. A man of that kind must not expect the Lord to give him anything; he is double-minded, and never can keep a steady course.

Jesus continues to work miracles in response to faith in our day too. I have been particularly impressed by the faith of some people who are in the healing ministry. They seem to perform again the type of miracles that we read Jesus performed in the Gospels and the apostles in Acts. Has it ever struck you that every time Jesus sent his apostles out to preach he gave them the power to heal and to work miracles—as if he linked the two ministries inextricably together, the ministry of healing and the ministry of preaching? In a sense, every preacher of the gospel has to be something of a miracle worker. And so it is significant that the only grace the apostles asked for, for themselves, besides the grace of boldness and courage in proclaiming the gospel was the grace of working miracles. After they are discharged from the court, they make this prayer:

And now, O Lord, mark their threats, and enable thy servants to speak thy word with all boldness. Stretch out thy hand to heal and cause signs and wonders to be done through the name of thy holy servant Jesus.

Their prayer seems to have been generously answered:

When they had ended their prayer, the building where they were assembled rocked, and all were filled with the Holy Spirit and spoke the word of God with boldness.

Acts 4:31

And many remarkable and wonderful things took place among the people at the hands of the apostles. In the end the sick were actually carried out into the streets and laid there on beds and stretchers, so that even the shadow of Peter might fall on one or another as he passed by; and the people from the towns round Jerusalem flocked in, bringing those who were ill or harassed by unclean spirits, and all of them were cured.

Acts 5:12, 15–16

St. Paul, who stands out as a wonder worker in Acts, will appeal to his power to perform miracles when he strives to establish his credentials as apostle in the early Church.

I am being very foolish, but it was you who drove me to it; my credentials should have come from you. In no respect did I fall short of these superlative apostles, even if I am a nobody. The marks of a true apostle were there, in the work I did among you, which called for such constant fortitude, and was attended by signs, marvels, and miracles.

2 Corinthians 12:11–12

Why do we not witness today the kinds of miracles that the early Church witnessed? Why are there such few miraculous healings, even raisings from the dead? Some say it is because there is no need for miracles today. My own feeling is that we have never needed miracles so badly; and the reason why we don't have more is that we just don't expect miracles to happen; our faith is very low. I recollect speaking with a Jesuit confrere who is doing excellent work among Hindus, by whom he is revered as a holy man and guru. He felt the call to launch out and proclaim the faith and explicit allegiance to the Risen Lord to his Hindu "disciples." But how to do this to a group of people who see all religions as equally good and who will wholeheartedly accept Jesus—but on their terms, as just another manifestation of the divinity, like Buddha or Krishna? I said to him, "Do you know when things will start to happen? When a daughter of one of your disciples dies, and you walk into the house and say to everyone, 'Do not weep; the girl will live. In the name of Jesus Christ, the Risen Lord, I shall bring her back to life,' and then proceed to make good your bold claim as the apostles did in Acts. That is when things will begin to happen, I assure you. There will be conversions to Jesus Christ and there will be hostility and persecution." Today we have very little of either in India.

I told you before that Jesus somehow linked the charism of healing and working miracles with the ministry of preaching. He, himself, joined the two things in his own life and apostolate, and he joined the two whenever he commissioned his Apostles to go out and preach. This is probably because for most of us nothing is so real as our bodies, and when we see God operating in our bodies then he becomes more real to us than ever.

The modern world, fortunately, has its share too of the mighty works of the Risen Lord still living in our midst. I know of missionaries who have performed miracles for their people. I am much impressed by the faith of a man like David Wilkerson who in his admirable book *The Cross and the Switchblade* tells us how he cures drug addicts whom modern medicine and modern psychiatry have given up as incurable. You can apparently do nothing for the addict who has begun to inject the drug into his bloodstream. Wilkerson claims he cures them by merely laying hands on them and communicating to them the power of the Holy Spirit. Here is faith in action for you!

If you want to learn of some other instances of outstanding faith, read the book *Realities* by Basilea Schlink and *God's Smuggler* by Brother Andrew, particularly the part about his seminary training where people are sent out on preaching expeditions with no more than a pound sterling in their pockets to put the gospel literally to the test before going out to preach it themselves.

If in our own lives we never or hardly ever experience God's miraculous interventions, it is either because we are not living dangerously enough or because our faith has grown dim and we hardly expect any miracles to occur. How important it is that there be miracles in our lives if we are to preserve a keen consciousness of God's presence and power. A miracle, in the religious sense, is not necessarily an event that contravenes the laws of nature—this would be a physical phenomenon that need not have any religious significance. For a miracle to occur in my life it is enough for me to have the deep conviction that what occurred was produced by God, that it was a direct intervention of God on my behalf. Any religion that postulates a personal God must of necessity give great importance to two things: petitionary prayer and miracles. God becomes personal to me when I cry out to him, when I see no hope in any human being, and when he personally intervenes to deliver me or to give me strength or to enlighten and guide me. If he did not do this he would not be personal to *me* because he would not be an active factor in my life.

Today we seem to be losing this sense of God's constant intervention in our lives. The Jews of the Bible had a tremendous sense for this. That is why they were a people of great faith. Did it rain? Then it was God who made it rain; they very conveniently overlooked the atmospheric changes that brought them the rain. Did they win or lose in battle? It was God who made them win or lose. It hardly occurred to them to credit the results of battle to the skill or the negligence of their generals. Even if their troops displayed cowardice on the battlefield and were therefore routed, it was God who weakened the hearts of the soldiers by taking away their courage. All their attention was focused on the Primary Cause, on God. They seem to have just overlooked secondary causes. And so, in everything, it was natural for them to have recourse to God.

With us it is just the opposite. Do you have a headache? There is no point in getting down on your knees and praying. Take an aspirin. Humankind has come of age. Instead of spending our time in Church praying, let us build laboratories, rely on our own ingenuity, and invent the medicines and other things we need. All of this has a point; but it is not the full truth. We have become so conscious of secondary causes that God no longer features in our life and our thinking. It is perfectly true that aspirin needs inventing, but it is God who gives us the motivation to invent it. It is also true that the aspirin rids you of your headache, but the full truth is that it is God who cures you through that aspirin tablet, his almighty power at work within the healing or soothing forces of aspirin. God is as much a need in every event and action of our modern lives and our modern cities as he was to the Jews in the desert. We have just lost the faith-sense that enables us to see him operating behind every secondary cause, to see his hand guiding events personally through the veil of human agencies.

I remember reading an article some years ago written by two lay psychiatrists. It was a study on priests and religious whom they had treated. They remarked that out of the dozens of priests and brothers who came to them for help in their personal problems, only two ever even so much as mentioned the name of God in all their interviews, and only one of these, a lay brother, mentioned

him as an important factor in his life and his cure. To all the rest it
seemed as though God had no part in their lives. He was never re-
ferred to when they were talking about problems that were most
intimate to them. Isn't this a sign of how much God has receded
into the background of our lives? How weak our sense of faith has
become! We just don't expect God to intervene powerfully and directly in our lives. Do we have a psychological problem? Then a
psychiatrist is needed. A physical illness? Call a doctor. Jesus seemed
to think quite otherwise. The baker was surely an important factor
to him in the obtaining of our daily bread, but the most important
factor was our heavenly Father, and it was to him we had to turn
to ask for our daily bread.

If we do not have faith, we shall not even think of turning to
God in all our needs. If we do not have faith, our prayers will be
ineffective even if we turn to God. Tell me, supposing you were to
make a long list of petitions and place them before your Father in
heaven, would you be surprised if they were all granted? Why?
Were you not just taking for granted that you would get all you
asked for? Doesn't your surprise show a deficiency in your faith?

Faith is not something you can produce. Don't *force* yourself to
have faith—it wouldn't be faith at all but a strained effort to make
yourself believe. Faith comes as a gift from just exposing yourself to
God's company. The more you deal with God the more you begin
to realize that nothing is impossible to him. You will begin to have
the faith that makes you convinced that he can change stones into
children of Abraham. Then you will be convinced that he can easily change your stony heart too, and the moment that conviction
sets in, the change in your heart will begin.

This then is the first law of petitionary prayer. Prayer must be
accompanied by an unshakable faith. Remember, "You need only
say to this mountain, 'Be lifted from your place and hurled into the
sea,' and what you say will be done. And whatever you pray for in
faith, you will receive." Those problems of yours that seem like

enormous mountains will yield before the power of your faith. Jesus adds a very interesting detail in Mark 11:24: "I tell you, then, whatever you ask for in prayer, believe that you *have* received it, and it *will* be yours." How strange. Believe that you have received it and it *will* be yours. It is not yet yours, but you must pray as if it is yours already. That is the reason why some people blend their petition with thanksgiving. They will pray for something; then they begin to thank God for having granted them what they were asking for. What is the proper time to begin thanksgiving? Obviously, you will say, when you have received what you are asking for. But no! The proper time to begin thanksgiving is when God has given you the conviction that he has heard your prayer—even before you actually receive the gift you were asking for. When friends give you a check, do you first wait to have it cashed in the bank before you thank them? When you realize that God is going to give you what you are asking for, that is the moment to begin to thank him. I read of a woman who prayed to be cured of arthritis. She began her thanksgiving three whole years before the cure came, because she was convinced that the cure was on its way. So when we pray, we must be attuned to what God is saying to us and receive the promise of the gift before the gift comes. Could this be what St. Paul meant when he told the Philippians to blend their petitions with thanksgiving?

> The Lord is near; have no anxiety, but in everything make your requests known to God in *prayer and petition with thanksgiving.* Then the peace of God, which is beyond our utmost understanding, will keep guard over your hearts and your thoughts, in Christ Jesus.
>
> Philippians 4:6–7

That, incidentally, is a beautiful formula for always living in the peace of God!

The Second Law of Prayer: Forgiveness

In Mark 11, Jesus tells us of the need for faith if our prayers are to be effective. In that same passage, he insists on the need of something else: forgiveness.

> And when you stand praying, if you have a grievance against anyone, forgive him, so that your Father in heaven may forgive you the wrongs you have done.
>
> Mark 11:25

This is a fundamental law of all prayer, something Jesus insists on again and again. If you do not forgive, you will not be forgiven; it is impossible for you to be united with God.

> If, when you are bringing your gift to the altar, you suddenly remember that your brother has a grievance against you, leave your gift where it is before the altar. First go and make your peace with your brother, and only then come back and offer your gift.
>
> Matthew 5:23–24

Here is the principal reason why the prayer of so many people is lacking in power: they nurse resentments within their hearts. I have frequently been amazed to see the weight of resentment that people, even priests and religious, carry with them through life: resentments against superiors, particularly for injustices, real or imaginary. They are not aware of the harm that this does to their prayer life, to their apostolic effectiveness and, in many instances, even to their physical health.

These sentiments of bitterness, hatred, and rancor poison our system and cause us suffering. And yet it is amazing to see how we cling to them. Sometimes we would rather part with any possession, no matter how precious, than with a grudge we are nursing against someone. We simply refuse to forgive! Jesus will have none of this. His teaching is unambiguous: If you do not forgive, I shall have nothing to do with you!

I therefore suggest that right from the start of this retreat you spend time ferreting out any resentments you have and getting rid of them. If you don't, your prayer during this retreat is bound to suffer. Don't hesitate to give it all the time you need, even if you spend two or three whole days just on this. I advise you to make a list of all the people whom you hate or hold a grudge against or refuse to love and forgive. Making this list may not be as easy as it sounds for some of you. If there is one sentiment that we priests are in the habit of repressing, after sexual feelings, it is hate feelings. And so we sometimes meet priests who will tell you in all sincerity that they hate no one and love everyone, but who, unconsciously, betray their resentments and bitterness in their way of speaking and acting. One simple way of unearthing repressed resentments that you might have is to make a list of people you are negatively inclined to. If that doesn't yield results, make a list of the people you have a poor opinion of, or even those whom you like less than others, or, finally, those who dislike *you*. The list may yield some surprises in the way of ill feelings or resentments you may be harboring.

Getting Anger out of Your System

What are you to do with that list? I wouldn't have you jump to forgiveness too soon. This might lead only to further repression of your resentful feelings. It is frequently a help to deal with resentments by "getting them out of your system." The ideal would be to talk things over with the person you resent and express your resentments to him or her quite frankly. This ideal, unfortunately, is not always attainable, either because the persons in question are not around or because, even though they are around, they just wouldn't be able to respond to your expression of resentment in a constructive way.

The next best thing then is to express your resentment in fantasy. Imagine you see this person you resent in front of you and really "tell him off." Forgiveness is not weakness or cowardice. I know a priest who just couldn't bring himself to forgive and to trust a colleague whom he resented. For months on end he had prayed for the grace of forgiveness, to no apparent effect. When I finally got him to "have it out," to confront this person in the presence of a third party who served as a skilled catalyst, forgiveness came so easily that he even wondered if there was anything to forgive. Another priest was having trouble forgiving a subordinate who had caused him much suffering by calumniating him. The feeling of resentment rankled him for months and would almost invariably crop up in prayer, however much he tried to push it out of his mind. I got him to confront this person in imagination through a roleplaying session, even to express his hurt and anger by pounding a pillow. After the session he realized what a coward he had been, how weak he had been in dealing with this subordinate of his. The situation did not change. The calumniating continued. But this priest was now emotionally able to understand and forgive this person. He had got the anger out of his system and it troubled him no longer.

I can see how, in both these instances, a too hasty recourse to prayer might have aggravated rather than alleviated the problem. And so, while I earnestly recommend the forms of prayer I am about to outline here as a means to forgiving others, I must warn you that they may not always be a substitute for the deep-rooted emotional (sometimes even physical) need we have for getting the hostility out of our system.

How to Forgive through Prayer

That clear, here are some effective ways of obtaining the grace to forgive and to get rid of resentments:

1. Pray for the welfare of the people you dislike. This is what Jesus recommended in the sermon on the Mount. As you keep praying for them, your attitude toward them undergoes a mysterious change. You begin to care, to be positively inclined, even to love them. It is easier to forgive people we love and pray for.

2. See every injustice done to you as planned and controlled by God for some mysterious purpose. It is not enough to say, "God permitted it." God does not just "permit" things; he plans them, he controls them. The passion of Christ, that enormous act of human injustice, was not just permitted by God. It was planned and willed and foreordained. And so Jesus will be constantly talking about having to go through his passion so that "the Scriptures may be fulfilled." And St. Peter says in Acts 2:22–23,

I speak of Jesus of Nazareth, a man singled out by God. . . . When he had been given up to you, by the deliberate will and plan of God, you used heathen men to crucify and kill him.

If we look upon all the "passions" in our own lives—that is, all the injustices, real or imaginary, done to us—as Jesus looked upon his as controlled and foreordained by God, as his deliberate will and plan, we will not dwell long or deeply on secondary causes, on the people who caused us hurt and pain, on the Herods and Pilates in our lives. We will look beyond them at the Father who holds all the strings of our lives in his hands and who has ordained this suffering for our good and the good of the world, and we will find it easier to forgive our persecutors and our enemies.

However, this may lead to a further problem. Our resentments may get displaced onto God! Because of our habit of repressing sentiments of hatred and rage, we priests sometimes find it hard to understand how people can develop very deep-seated resentments against God when a calamity occurs in their lives: the death of a loved person, the loss of health, financial misfortune, etc. These people understand rightly that in some mysterious fashion the Lord "is to blame," that he is behind all of these events. And even though their faith and understanding will tell them that the Lord has planned all of this for their good, their heart and their emotions cannot help resenting the person who has ordained these calamities when he could have prevented them. My mind may tell me that the surgeon's knife is for my good, but that doesn't prevent my body from resisting it and hating it as an evil—so it is with the heart that cannot always be ruled by the head in what it feels.

When resentments against God come to the surface, it is good to give expression to them in his presence—to give expression to all the anger and hatred you feel. And don't be bothered about the language you use. I remember doing this once: I was deeply disappointed at not getting something I very much wanted, and I resented God for not giving it to me. I resented him to the point of refusing to talk to him, refusing to pray, for two whole days. Childish, if you will, but effective. I knew deep down that I could trust God enough to express my resentments to him, just as I am in the habit of doing with my friends. I have no fear to express all my negative feelings to them because I am so sure that they love me enough to understand, and that as a result of this "encounter," the love between us will grow. If I withheld my negative feelings from them, I would be treating them politely, as acquaintances rather than intimate friends, and I would expose myself to the danger of cooling off in my relationships with them, for resentments cannot always be "willed" away; they have a habit of rankling under the surface and undermining our love in the long run.

You need not be afraid to say angry, even bitter words to God. As holy a person as Job did this. This did not indicate at all that he was lacking in respect for the Lord. On the contrary, it was a sign of his intimacy with God. And it is significant that in the end the Lord praises and commends him while he rebukes Job's friends who were so scandalized by Job's bitter words and who were urging him to blame himself rather than the Lord for all his misfortunes. As we vent all our negative feelings against the Lord, they will gradually be drained off. Our love will come to the surface and we will be happy to find that this "quarrel" we had with him has not only not undermined our relationship with him, it has deepened it. After all, even in expressing anger to people, I am contacting them and showing them I care enough to be angry. If my relationship with you is fragile and I am unsure of it, I shall be very reluctant to show you my anger for fear of losing you. I need to be sure enough of you and intimate enough with you to trust you with an expression of my anger against you. Anger is very frequently the obverse side of love, frequently love itself in other form. The opposite of love is not anger or even hate. It is coldness and indifference.

3. Here is something else you can do to rid yourself of grievances and resentments. Stand in spirit before the Crucified Christ and keep your eyes fixed on this great Victim of injustice. It won't be long before you feel ashamed that you are making such a fuss about the little injustices you have been subjected to—you who call yourself his disciple and who agreed to follow him, precisely on the understanding that you too would take up your cross as he did.

I have known people who practiced this exercise to feel not only shame at their harboring resentments, but even joy and gladness that they were accounted worthy to suffer something of the fate of their Master. It would be wonderful if you were to reach that stage yourself. Then you will understand something of what he said in his sermon on the Mount,

How blest are those who have suffered persecution for the
cause of right . . . how blest you are, when you suffer insults
and persecution and every kind of calumny for my sake. Accept it with gladness and exultation.

Matthew 5:10–12

You will also understand the secret of the saints who felt such
joy when they were humiliated without giving any cause for the
humiliation, and such gratitude toward their "persecutors" whom
they looked upon as benefactors! Now make sure you do not force
these feelings upon yourself. If you do, they won't last and will only
leave you discouraged and resentful again. Enough for you to stay
close to your Crucified Master and to understand that the injustices
you have been subjected to are part of the price you pay for following him closely. Someday, as you come closer to him, he will
give you the grace to find joy in crucifixion and to break out in
praise and song, rather than in bitter angry words.

In all of these exercises, for attaining the ability to forgive, I
have assumed that you are the innocent victim of injustice. In most
cases, however, this is too much to assume. We are very frequently
responsible, at least in some degree, for the injustices that come our
way. Only we find it very hard to accept, or even see, that responsibility. I am hopeful that once we have got our resentments and
negative feelings out and had recourse to prayer, it will be easier to
forgive if forgiveness is called for.

I have shared with you thus far two of the laws that govern the
art of prayer. There are yet other laws, but I shall leave them for
another conference for fear that this conference be drawn out too
long. It seems to me that none of the other laws have the immense
value that these two have, for nothing is so important to prayer as
faith and forgiveness. I offered you some exercises in forgiveness
and have explained to you the importance of faith, so you have
enough "employment" for the hours of prayer that you have ahead
of you. I exhort you to accept Jesus' words on the power and ef-

fectiveness of prayer with the simplicity of a little child—and then the kingdom of heaven will open to you. I wish to end this conference on a moving story that Ramakrishna would tell his disciples to illustrate this simple childlike faith that the Lord expects of us when we approach him in prayer.

In a village in Bengal there lived a poor widow whose only son had to go to school to a neighboring village each day. The boy had to traverse a jungle each day to go to school; so he said, "Mother, I'm afraid to go through that jungle alone. Send someone with me." The mother replied, "We are too poor, son, to afford a servant who could accompany you to and from school. Ask your brother Krishna to accompany you to school. He is the Lord of the jungle and he will listen to your prayer." That is just what the little fellow proceeded to do. He walked up to the jungle next day and called out to his brother Krishna. And the Lord replied, "What do you want, son?" Said the boy, "Will you come with me to school each day and accompany me back home through this jungle? I'm afraid to go alone." "Yes," said the Lord Krishna, "it will give me much pleasure to do that for you." And so Krishna would wait for his little protégé each morning and evening and walk with him through the jungle.

Now when the schoolmaster's birthday came, all the children were expected to bring him a birthday present. The widow said to her son, "We are too poor to afford a birthday present for your master, son. Ask your brother Krishna to give you a present for him." Krishna gave the boy a jug full of milk and the boy marched proudly to the schoolmaster's house and placed the jug at his feet together with the many other presents that were laid out there. But the master paid no attention to this humble offering, and after a while the child began to whimper with the spontaneity of children, "Nobody is paying any attention to my present. Nobody is noticing my present." Until the master said to his servant, "For heavens' sake take that jug into the kitchen or we shall never hear the end of this complaining." The servant emptied the contents of the jug into a bowl and was going to return the jug to the boy when, to his amazement, he noticed the jug was filled with milk again. He emptied it again into the large bowl, and it filled up again under his astonished eyes—just like that phial of oil that the widow used for the prophet Elisha.

When the master heard of this miracle, he called the boy and said, "Where did you get this jug from?" "Brother Krishna gave it to me," said the lad. "Brother Krishna? Who is this brother Krishna of yours?" "He is the Lord of the Jungle. He accompanies me to and from school each day." The master was incredulous. "We're all coming to see this brother Krishna of yours," he said, and he and the servants and the other students all marched our little boy to the edge of the jungle and said, "Call your brother Krishna. We want to see him."

So the boy began to call to Krishna, "Brother Krishna . . . Brother Krishna . . ." But the Lord who had always come so promptly in the past at the sound of his little friend, was silent today. The jungle was silent. All that could be heard was the echo of the boy calling out to his brother Krishna in vain. At last the poor fellow was reduced to tears, "Brother Krishna, please come," he said. "If you don't come they will not believe me. They're saying I'm a liar. Do come, brother Krishna." Then, at last, he heard the voice of the Lord who said, "Son, I cannot come. The day your master has your childlike faith and your simple, pure heart, I shall come."

I was much moved when I first read this story, because it reminded me of Jesus' dealings with his disciples. Only those who had faith were to see him risen. We say, let him first appear to me and then I shall believe. Or else how will I know if this is real or just the effect of autosuggestion? The Lord doesn't seem interested in helping us with that problem. He says, "First believe and then you will see. Only believe and nothing will be impossible to you."

6

Petitionary Prayer and Its Laws

Among the writings of the Desert Fathers there is a set of homilies attributed to Macarius of Egypt. There is a very delightful homily among these, one in which Macarius claims that even the greatest sinner can aspire to become a mystic provided he turns away from his sin and trusts in the Lord. Here is an encouraging paragraph from that sermon:

> For even a baby, too weak for anything and unable to walk to his mother on his own little feet, can yet roll about and scream and cry because he wants her. Then the mother is sorry for him, and at the same time pleased that the little one desires her so much. Therefore, as he cannot come to her, she, moved by his longings and by her own love of her child, takes him up and sweetly fondles and feeds him. Thus also deals the loving God with the soul who comes to him and longs for him.

By that comparison of the little child Macarius captures admirably Jesus' doctrine on prayer. There is hope for all of us. God isn't asking questions about our worthiness or unworthiness. He isn't looking into our past life with its failures and infidelities. It is enough that (a) we are crying out for him and we want him very much, (b) we are helpless to attain what we want, and (c) we believe he will do for us what we cannot do for ourselves.

The Power of Prayer: Narada

Hindu literature contains some fine stories that could serve as illustrations of Jesus' doctrine. One of them tells of the sage Narada who was on his way to the temple of the Lord Vishnu. At night he stopped at a certain village where a poor villager and his wife made him welcome. When the villager learned that Narada was on a pilgrimage to the temple of Vishnu, he said to him, "Will you pray to the Lord that we be given children? My wife and I greatly desire children but the Lord has not yet given them to us." Narada promised he would intercede for them, set out again, reached the temple and placed the petition of that villager before the Lord Vishnu. The Lord was abrupt. He said, "It is not in the destiny of that man to have children." Narada bowed to this statement of the Lord and returned home. Five years later he set out again on pilgrimage to that temple. Once again he sought and was gladly given hospitality in the house of that simple villager. This time, however, he was surprised to see three little children playing in the courtyard. "Whose children are those?" asked Narada. "Mine," said the villager. Said Narada, "So the Lord did give you children after all?" "Yes," said the villager, "a little after you left us, five years ago, a saint passed by this village. He gave his blessing to me and my wife and prayed over us. The Lord heard his prayer and gave us these three lovely children you see here." Narada was dumbfounded and couldn't wait to get to the Lord's temple the next day. When he got there the first thing he said to the Lord was, "Didn't you tell me it was not in the destiny of that man to have children? How is it then that he has three children now?" When the Lord Vishnu heard that he laughed aloud and said, "That must be the doing of a saint. Saints have the power to change destiny!"

A quaint story, isn't it? I thought so too, until I suddenly remembered a similar story. "Woman, my hour has not yet come." Then, mysteriously, his hour did come and he worked the miracle of changing water into wine. Didn't Mary show there the power of petitionary prayer to change destiny? In James 5:16–18 we read,

> A good man's prayer is powerful and effective. Elijah was a man with human frailties like our own; and when he prayed earnestly that there should be no rain, not a drop fell in the land for three years and a half; then he prayed again, and down came the rain and the land bore crops once more.

There's a story very similar to the story of Narada in the Second Book of Kings, Chapter 20: Hezekiah fell sick, and was at death's door; indeed, the prophet Isaiah visited him with this message from the Lord: "Put thy affairs in order; it is death that awaits thee, not recovery." At this Hezekiah turned his face toward the wall, and prayed to the Lord thus: "Remember, Lord, I entreat thee, a life that has kept true to thee, an innocent heart; how I did ever what was thy will." And Hezekiah wept bitterly. Whereupon, before ever Isaiah reached the middle of the courtyard, the word of the Lord came to him: "Go back and tell Hezekiah, the ruler of my people, here is a message to thee from the Lord, the God of thy father David. I have listened to thy prayer, and marked thy tears; be it so, I have granted thee recovery. Within three days thou shalt be on thy way to the Lord's temple, and I will add fifteen years to thy life." Here is another instance of the power of prayer to change destiny. What could be more definitive than a word of the Lord sent through his prophet? How does one appeal against that? How can one make the Lord change his mind? And yet prayer does the impossible. Nothing is impossible to God; so nothing is impossible to petitionary prayer made to God as Jesus taught us to make it.

I frequently come up against this objection raised by my retreatants: How is it possible to make God change his mind? The will of God is unchangeable. That is a philosophical objection to which I have no solution. I can no more explain how prayer can change the mind of God than I can explain how God became human or how Christ is present in the Blessed Sacrament. These are mysteries that our human mind will never be able to grasp satisfactorily. It is enough for us to know that Jesus told us clearly that what we ask for will be given us. He did not expect us to acquiesce fatalistically to what we consider to be "destiny" or "the mind of God"; he wanted us to ask and receive, to seek and find, to knock and have the door opened to us. So it is enough for us to launch out and discover to our wonder and delight that, philosophical objections notwithstanding, the doctrine of Jesus on prayer is true and that prayer works, as it did for Mary in Cana and for Ezechias when confronted with Isaias' prophecy.

Again and again the Bible gives us examples of this great mystery that God delights to have his mind changed by the prayers of his friends. Listen to what the prophet Amos says.

> This was a vision the Lord God showed me; here were locusts a-making, just at the time when the aftergrowth was coming up, after the king's crop had been carried. Short work had these made of all the land yielded; Ah, Lord God, said I, be merciful! How should Jacob survive, the puny creature he is? *And with that, the Lord relented:* Happen it shall not, said he. And a second vision the Lord God showed me, how he would summon them to ordeal by fire; fire should devour the waters below the earth, and devoured some part of them were. Ah, Lord God, said I, for pity! How should Jacob survive, the puny creature he is? *And with that, the Lord relented again:* Happen it shall not, said he.
>
> Amos 7:1–6

Moses has a lengthy argument with God in Exodus 32 and finally succeeds in making God change his mind.

The Lord said to Moses, I know them now for a stiff-necked race; spare me thy importunacy, let me vent my anger and destroy them; I will make thy posterity into a great nation instead. But Moses would still plead with the Lord his God. . . . *So the Lord relented*, and spared his people the punishment he had threatened.

Genesis 18:16–32 shows us Abraham attempting to do the same thing with God by interceding for the cities of Sodom and Gomorrha.

And the Lord said, should I hide my purpose from Abraham, this man who is destined to give birth to a people so great and so powerful? . . . So the Lord told him, The ill repute of Sodom and Gomorrah goes from bad to worse, their sin is grievous out of all measure. . . . Abraham drew close to him, and asked, Wilt thou, then sweep away the innocent with the guilty? Suppose there are fifty innocent men in the city, must they too perish? Wilt thou not spare the place to save fifty such innocent men that dwell there? . . . And the Lord told him, if I find fifty innocent citizens in Sodom, I will spare the whole place to save them. . . . Then he said, Lord, do not be angry with me for pleading thus; what if thirty are found there? If I find thirty, he said, I will not do it. I have taken it upon me, said he, to speak to my Lord, and speak I will; what if twenty are found there? If I find twenty, I will grant it life, he said, to save twenty. And he said, do not be angry with me, Lord, I entreat thee, for making one more plea still; what if ten are found there? I will spare it from destruction, he said, to save ten.

All our philosophical objections notwithstanding, the Bible shows us a God who leaves himself wide open to being influenced by the prayers of those he loves; a God who will reveal his plans to his prophets precisely so that they will make him change his mind and his plans through the power of their prayers; a God who has, by his own decree, subjected himself to the mighty force of persistent prayer.

The "Theology" of Petitionary Prayer

Petition was the only form of prayer that Jesus taught his disciples; it is, in fact, almost the only form of prayer that is taught explicitly in the entire Bible. This will sound strange to those of us who have been brought up on the notion that prayer is of different types and that adoration takes first place; petition, being a "selfish" form of prayer, takes last place. We have almost felt, haven't we, that sooner or later we must "out-grow" this inferior form of prayer and ascend to contemplation and love and adoration.

And yet, if we will reflect, we will find that there is barely any form of prayer, adoration and love very much included, that is not contained in petitionary prayer that is properly made. Petition teaches us our total dependence on God. It teaches us to trust in him totally. Some people say. "Our heavenly Father knows everything that I need. And if he looks after the birds of the air and the lilies of the field, he will surely look after me. Jesus told us this quite explicitly. So I don't spend my time asking the Father for what he already knows I need and wants to give me anyway." The doctrine in that statement is correct; the conclusion is inaccurate. Jesus does tell us that his Father looks after the birds of the air and the lilies of the field. But the conclusion he draws is not, Don't ask, (for he himself is constantly urging us to ask) but, Don't worry! Can there be anything more absurd (following the logic given above) than that we should pray for laborers to be sent into the harvest of the Lord? It is the Lord's harvest. He knows that laborers are needed. And he surely wants to send them to his harvest field. And yet he insists that we pray that those laborers be sent. Once again we come up against this attitude of God who has willed to be subjected to the power of prayer, even to the extent of seeming to *need* the prayers of people for his power to be unleashed. So, once again, trust in the Lord does not mean abandoning petitionary prayer. It means making your petition known to God; make sure you do that! And then leaving everything to him, confident that he will take charge of everything and will make everything come out right. So no need to worry any more. St. Paul puts it admirably:

> The Lord is near; have no anxiety, but in everything make your requests known to God in prayer and petition with thanksgiving. Then the peace of God, which is beyond our utmost understanding, will keep guard over your hearts and your thoughts in Christ Jesus.
>
> Philippians 4:6–7

I have already explained to you something of the theology of petitionary prayer in the previous conference, something of the reason why petition and miracles are necessary. They make God real in our lives. He is an active, intervening, caring God, not a distant deity with whom we could not interact in the practical destiny of our lives. There is yet another reason for the importance Jesus gave to petitionary prayer. It is summed up in this sentence: "Without me you can do nothing." Through the ceaseless use of petitionary prayer and through constantly experiencing its effect in our lives we come to realize our dependence on God, our need for him, experientially. We are forced to "live" this need for God.

The Council of Trent expressed this theology well when it said, "God does not command us to do what is impossible, but to do what is possible to us and ask for what is impossible." The Council of Orange was more detailed and explicit: "If our thoughts are righteous and our steps avoid sin, it is by the gift of God; for every time an action of ours is good, it is God who acts in us and with us, causing us to act" (Canon 9). "Even those who have been born to a new life, even those who are made whole, must *always implore the divine assistance* to be able to attain their final perfection, or simply to persevere in good" (Canon 10). "Everything that man has of truth and goodness comes from this divine spring; we must always thirst after it in this desert so that, refreshed as by a gentle rain, we may have strength not to fail on the way" (Canon 22).

The Christian must be deeply convinced that religion is not something we *do*, not even something we do for God. Religion is what God does for us and in us and through us, so that even our efforts and desires and "cooperation with grace" is a gift of God. Simone Weil was so wise when she said that the trouble with the Marxists (and, for that matter, with all humanists who limit themselves to human beings and their potential and have no place for God) is that they expect to mount up in the air by dint of marching inexorably forward. Marching forward will sooner or later bring you back to the point from where you started. All your marching, no matter how vigorous, will not succeed in raising you even one foot up into the air. For that, God's intervention is needed. And Jesus made sure we always kept an awareness of this by insisting that we ceaselessly ask God for everything, just everything, even for the coming of his kingdom, for laborers in his harvest field, yes, even for our simple material needs and our daily bread. If we did this oftener, we would taste that "peace of God that is beyond our utmost understanding" of which Paul speaks.

I earnestly recommend that you read Paul's letters to the Romans and the Galatians these days; you will find there the whole theology of petitionary prayer admirably exposed, because he develops there, in masterful fashion, the theology of our total dependence on God. We must become little children in God's presence. A little boy does not "earn" his keep; his parents love him and he merits their love and care and their concern for providing all his needs, not because of what he *does* but because of what he *is*—their child. He has only to manifest his needs to have them met by his loving parents. There is nothing more pathetic than to have a child worried and anxious about his growth and development and survival—a child who attempts to grow by stretching himself rather than by trustingly leaning on his parents.

Now I wouldn't have you go away with the notion that this is a lazy theology, that prayer dispenses us from effort, even strenuous effort. Pray to God and quit worrying does not mean don't work hard to obtain what you expect God to give you. The Lord feeds the birds of the air, no doubt, but he doesn't drop food into upturned beaks. He expects the birds to search for it, to make every effort to get what he is giving them. The secret here is to work as though everything depended on us and to trust in God as though everything depended on him. This is a difficult combination to achieve. Those who work hard are soon tempted to rely on their own efforts rather than on God's blessing and grace. Let builders of houses toil ceaselessly, let them see to every single detail, leaving nothing to chance; and let them be keenly aware, all along, that unless the Lord builds they will build in vain. Let the city authorities use all the means in their power to protect and guard their city. But let them have a keen sense of the fact that it is the Lord who guards them, not all the technological devices they have invented. We use these devices, these human means, all of them, but we do not trust in them; we do not lean on them. Our trust is only in the Lord. Human means are necessary, but they are also inadequate. We must develop the ability to sense the Lord's power operating behind them.

7

More Laws
of Prayer

In the previous conference I started to give you what I called the
"laws of prayer" and broke off after I gave you the first two, faith
and forgiveness. Here are four more.

1. Unworldliness
James 4:2ff. says,

> You do not get what you want, because you do not pray for it.
> Or, if you do, your requests are not granted because you pray
> from wrong motives, to spend what you get on your pleasures.
> You false, unfaithful creatures! Have you never learned that
> love of the world is enmity to God? Whoever chooses to be the
> world's friend makes himself God's enemy.

Pleasure seekers cannot expect God to become a partner to
their lust for pleasure. The desire for pleasure, even for sense pleasure, is a good thing. Life would be colorless and drab without it.
What is reprehensible is the inordinate craving for pleasure, the
hankering after luxuries and superfluities, the cult of money, which
can bring us these things.

Jesus advocates a life that is simple, uncluttered by luxuries and wealth. He bids us ask for our daily bread, our daily sustenance, not for the superfluities that glut our consumer-society markets. He is very conscious of the dangers of riches and even goes to the extent of saying that a man who loves money has thereby automatically ceased to love God; the two loves just cannot coexist in a human heart.

So if these are the things we are asking God for, we need not be surprised that he doesn't answer our prayers. Even more, if these are the things we are living for (even though we keep them out of our prayer) our prayers before the Lord are not likely to be powerful. Jesus would have us seek God's kingdom and his justice primarily, not the comforts and good things of this world.

2. Generosity

Those who expect God to be generous with them must be generous with their fellows. "Give," says Jesus, "and gifts will be given you. Good measure, pressed down, shaken together, and running over, will be poured into your lap; for whatever measure you deal out to others will be dealt to you in return" (Luke 6:38).

If you are tight-fisted and calculating with the poor, the needy, with those who ask you for help and service, how can you expect God to be generous with you?

3. Pray in Jesus' Name

This is a practice that Jesus enjoins on his apostles when he encourages them to ask his Father for the things they need.

> In truth, in very truth I tell you, he who has faith in me will do what I am doing; and he will do greater things still because I am going to the Father. Indeed *anything you ask in my name* I will do, so that the Father may be glorified in the Son. If you

ask anything in my name I will do it. . . . I appointed you to go on and bear fruit, fruit that shall last; so that the Father may give you *all that you ask in my name.* . . . When that day comes you will ask nothing of me. In very truth I tell you, if you ask the Father for anything *in my name,* he will give it you. So far you have asked nothing in my name. Ask and you will receive, that your joy may be complete.

John 14:12–14, 15:16, 16:23–24

It is from these words, no doubt, that the Church developed its practice of addressing prayers to the Father "through Jesus Christ Our Lord" and "in the name of Jesus Christ your Son." He would do well to imitate the Church here if we wish our prayers to be powerful before the Father. Praying in Jesus' name means relying on his influence with the Father, on his intercession, on the Father's love for him and eagerness to please him and give him all he asks for. It means having a great trust that whatever Jesus asks of the Father, the Father will surely give. It also means asking for things according to the mentality and the spirit of Jesus. To pray in Jesus' name then, would mean that we do not ask for things that he would not ask the Father for. He himself eschewed riches, honors, pomp, dignity. It is hard to see how we can ask for these things or for a surfeit of worldly pleasures if we are praying in his name.

4. Persistence

Of all the laws I have been enumerating here perhaps this one is, after faith and forgiveness, the most important and one that Jesus insisted on repeatedly. He tells us quite explicitly that it is not enough to ask for something once. We must persist in prayer; ask again and again, ceaselessly, tirelessly, until the Father listens to us and grants our petition. Listen to the two examples he gives us of persistent prayer.

The first is from Luke 11.

Suppose one of you has a friend who comes to him in the middle of the night and says, "My friend, lend me three loaves, for a friend of mine on a journey has turned up at my house, and I have nothing to offer him"; and he replies from inside, "Do not bother me. The door is shut for the night; my children and I have gone to bed; and I cannot get up and give you what you want." I tell you that even if he will not provide for him out of friendship, the very shamelessness of the request will make him get up and give him all he needs. And so I say to you, ask, and you will receive.

The refusal to take no for an answer; the shamelessness of his persistent asking. Jesus is positively urging us to pray like this man! He is saying, in effect, "Even though God seems to be turning a deaf ear to your prayer, don't give up. Be shameless. Be persistent. Keep knocking. Put pressure on him!"

We find the second example in Luke 18. This one was explicitly given by Jesus to inculcate perseverance and persistence in prayer.

He spoke to them in a parable to show that they should keep on praying and never lose heart: "There was once a judge who cared nothing for God or man, and in the same town there was a widow who constantly came before him demanding justice against her opponent. For a long time he refused; but in the end he said to himself, 'True, I care nothing for God or man; but this widow is so great a nuisance that I will see her righted before she wears me out with her persistence.' The Lord said, "You hear what the unjust judge says; and will not God vindicate his chosen, who cry out to him day and night, while he listens patiently to them?"

The message is clear enough. Can there be a more desperate situation than that of a poor widow with no influence, no strings to pull, confronted with a judge who is downright callous? Yet, even in a desperate situation like this one, persistence prayer triumphs. If it triumphs with a hard-hearted judge, how much more will it triumph with my tender-hearted Father? The reason why we frequently do not get what we are asking for is that we ask for a while and then tire of asking when we do not get what we are asking for right away. We must take the lesson that Jesus gives us to heart; become like the widow who was "so great a nuisance" and "wore the judge out with her persistence."

We have an admirable example of this doctrine in the Canaanite woman of Matthew 15, who persisted in spite of all rebuffs she got from Jesus.

> A Canaanite woman from those parts came crying out: "Sir! have pity on me, Son of David; my daughter is tormented by a devil." But he said not a word in reply. His disciples came and urged him: "Send her away; see how she comes shouting after us." Jesus replied, "I was sent to the lost sheep of the house of Israel, and to them alone." But the woman came and fell at his feet and cried, "Help me Sir." To this Jesus replied, "It is not right to take the children's bread and throw it to the dogs." "True, sir," she answered; "and yet the dogs eat the scraps that fall from their masters' table." Hearing this Jesus replied, "Woman, what faith you have! Be it as you wish!" And from that moment her daughter was restored to health.

The dialogue is too eloquent to need any comment. This is more like a stubborn struggle than prayer as we generally think of it. It reminds me of a story I once read of St. Anthony's successor, the abbot Sisoes, who, in his old age learned that one of his disciples, Abraham, had fallen into sin. He stood before God in prayer and said, "God, whether you like it or not, I shall not leave you alone unless you heal him." And his prayer was granted immediately! Shocking, until you realize that this is just what the Canaanite woman did, and Jesus actually admired her for it.

Petition: A Way of Life

The words of Jesus on prayer sound so simple: "Ask and you shall receive." Disarmingly simple. But behind that simple formula lies a whole way of life: a life of faith, of forgiveness of our brothers and sisters, of generosity with those in need, of unworldliness, of total trusting in and dependence on God. Petition is not just a form of prayer; it is a whole way of life. When we understand this, Jesus' words about the tremendous efficacy of prayer take on great credibility.

How much petition should we make? What place should we give to petitionary prayer in our prayer life? That is difficult to say. Each one must follow the promptings of the Spirit here. We must have a balanced diet in our prayer life with room for adoration, contemplation, various forms of prayer, meditation in its different forms, the sacraments, scripture reading, intercession and, of course, petition. The Spirit will lead us sometimes to emphasize one, sometimes another. Let us follow his lead and our own needs. One thing, however, is clear: we never "outgrow" the need for making simple petitionary prayer. No matter how much we progress in prayer and contemplation, no matter how holy we become, petitionary prayer will always be a duty incumbent upon us, one from which we may never dispense ourselves, for we shall always have to say, "Father in heaven, holy be your name, your kingdom come . . . give us today our daily bread, forgive us our sins, lead us not to the test." This is, indeed, the scandal of Christian prayer, the type of prayer Christ taught us: it is about the only form of prayer that makes no sense from a merely human-centred point of view. Meditation and reflection make sense. Contemplation, with its benefits of union with the divine and psychological growth, makes good sense. So does even adoration: the sense of awe and wonder and reverence before the Divine. But petition seems so senseless, so wasteful: puny human beings with their petitions standing before the unalterable plans of the Infinite! Human beings standing before God to ask for things like bread that they are perfectly capable of producing themselves—and that God himself expects them to produce by dint of their own efforts!

But no matter how meaningless petitionary prayer may seem to the philosopher, it begins to take on meaning to those who practice it assiduously, with child-like faith. Once you have discovered the power there is in prayer, you are not likely to be disturbed by philosophical difficulties connected with the why and wherefore. You have tried it out and it works. It brings you that "peace beyond understanding" that Paul speaks of, that "fullness of joy" that Jesus promised to those who exercised the prayer of petition. Having experienced this, you are quite content to continue asking for all you need, trusting that your heavenly Father loves you far more than any earthly father has ever loved his child.

Many priests today are said to be abandoning prayer. One simple reason for this is that they have never experienced the power that prayer brings. Those who have once experienced that prayer is power will never again abandon prayer for the rest of their lives. Mahatma Gandhi put it well: "I am telling you my own experience," he said, "and that of my colleagues: we could go for days on end without food; we could not live a single minute without prayer." Or, as he said another time, "Given the type of life I am leading, if I ceased to pray I should go mad!" If we ask God for so little it may well be because we feel the need for him so little. We are leading complacent, secure, well-protected, mediocre lives. We aren't living dangerously enough; we aren't living the way Jesus wanted us to live when he proclaimed the good news. The less we pray the less we are likely to live the risky, challenging life that the Gospels urge us to; the less of a challenge there is in our life, and the less we are likely to pray.

8

The Jesus Prayer

In this conference I wish to talk to you about a form of prayer that some of you may find somewhat bizarre. I confess I found it bizarre myself when I first got acquainted with it. I have since had plenty of time to discover its immense value in my life and in the lives of many people I have directed. Again and again I meet former retreatants who say to me, "The two things that have stayed with me after the retreat I made with you are the prayer of petition and the Jesus prayer." I know people who have discovered the continuous presence of God in their lives through the use of this prayer, and two persons whose spiritual director I am used this form of prayer and no other and experienced enormous changes in their lives only through the force of this prayer. I therefore share it with you with a feeling of confidence that it is bound to do an immense amount of good for at least some of you who are reading this—maybe most, or even all of you.

Let me begin by telling you how I first came in touch with this prayer. I was giving a conference to a group of sisters one evening and telling them how few are the books that really teach us to pray. Much of our classical literature on prayer (and I am afraid this applies to much of our modern literature as well—modern Catholic literature, that is. I have found Protestant literature in general to be more practical and unctional) deals with the nobility of prayer, the necessity of prayer, the theology of prayer, etc. Comparatively little of practical value is said on exactly how to go about the art of praying. That evening one of those sisters said to me, "I've discovered a book that deals exactly with the problem you mentioned this morning. It teaches you in a practical way how to pray. Would you care to read it?" I began reading the book after supper that evening and found it so fascinating that I stayed up late into the night in an attempt to finish it. The book was called *The Way of a Pilgrim*, written by an anonymous Russian pilgrim. The manuscript of this book was found in the cell of a monk of Mount Athos after his death, toward the beginning of this century. He might have been the author. The book soon became a spiritual classic and was translated into most modern languages. We have at least four Indian translations already, Hindi, Tamil, Malayalam, and Marathi.

The story of the pilgrim of this book is a simple one. He meets with all sorts of calamities, his wife and only child die. His house is burned down. Then he decides to give up the world and spend the rest of his life going on pilgrimages to various holy places. He sets out on his wanderings with a knapsack and a Bible and some bread in the knapsack. In his Bible reading he frequently finds exhortations to pray constantly, pray ceaselessly, pray day and night. This idea catches his fancy, and he starts to search for someone who will teach him to pray ceaselessly.

He runs into all sorts of persons, priests particularly. To his question, "How can I pray continuously, without interruption?" He gets all sorts of unsatisfactory answers. Says one, "Brother, only God can teach you to pray ceaselessly." Says another, "Do the will of God always. A man who always does God's will is thereby always praying." None of these answers satisfies the pilgrim, who takes the injunction to pray always quite literally. How, he wonders, can I pray at each moment whether awake or asleep when there are so many other things to occupy my mind? That's his problem: he thinks prayer is a matter of the mind; he has still to learn that prayer is done with the heart.

One day he runs into a monk who asks him where he is going

and what he is seeking. He replies, "I am going on a pilgrimage from one shrine to another. I am seeking someone who will teach me to pray ceaselessly." The monk, with the great assurance possessed by one who knows, says to him, "Brother, give great thanks to God, for at last he has sent you someone who will teach you to pray continuously. Come with me to my monastery!"

At the monastery the monk makes him sit in a little hut in the compound; he places a rosary in his hands, and says to him, "Say the following prayer five hundred times: 'Lord Jesus Christ, Son of God, have mercy on me, a miserable sinner.' " (I am not quite sure now about the number of times he was supposed to say that prayer. It was five hundred or one thousand—I don't remember, as it is years since I read that story.) The pilgrim soon said his prayer the appointed number of times, and he had time left over; but he did not dare disobey his spiritual father by saying the prayer more often than he had been commanded. The next day his spiritual father increased the number: one thousand. And it kept increasing each day: two thousand, three thousand, four thousand and so on. I remember having a group of sisters read this book in their refectory at meals during their retreat. Within a couple of days a number of them were quite tense and disturbed. "What's making you tense?" I said, during my private interviews with them. "That book," was the reply. "He's counting that prayer of his and he's got to four thousand. I can't stand the counting part!" That amused me. "If four thousand make you tense, just you wait till you have him saying it twenty thousand times. That will make you climb the walls!" It didn't! After the retreat those good sisters bought every copy of that book in the English language on the face of the earth! They had fallen in love with it and wanted to share it with their friends. And I had to wait for months on end before it saw another reprinting and I could get a copy for myself!

But let's get back to our pilgrim. He had barely got the habit of reciting this prayer thousands of times all through the day when his spiritual father died. The poor man accompanied the dead body to the grave and wept over his misfortune at losing this man whom the Lord had sent him and who had promised to teach him to pray continuously. There was no point in staying any further in the monastery. He picked up his knapsack and set out on his travels again. This time, however, in addition to his Bible, he had picked up a copy of the *Philokalia*, a book that contained excerpts of the writings of the Greek Fathers and doctors and theologians on this prayer that the Greeks call the Jesus Prayer.

Each day he would read passages from this book and follow its instructions religiously. From the book he learns to join the prayer to his breathing, so that when he breathes in he says, "Lord Jesus Christ, Son of God," and when he breathes out he says, "have mercy on me, a miserable sinner." Then, gradually, through some mysterious technique not described in the book and not to be applied to oneself without the explicit help of an experienced master, he "puts the prayer into his heart." Then one day, lo and behold, the heart takes over the prayer, and he is saying it continuously whether awake or asleep, whether eating or talking or walking. The heart just keeps reciting the prayer over and over again, as independent of the mind as it is in its beating all day long. So at last the pilgrim has learned the secret of continuous prayer. The rest of the book is dedicated to the adventures he meets with in his journeys, the miraculous effects of the prayer, and a good amount of doctrine, both on the prayer and on the spiritual life in general.

I must say that when I first read this book I found it charming as a piece of literature. It appealed to me for its sheer simplicity. But I was not so sure about the validity of its doctrine on prayer. I found the whole thing too mechanical, too much like autosuggestion. And I was initially inclined to forget all about it. However, I was also urged to give it a try for some days. So I began repeating a phrase, but not the one suggested by the book. You don't have to stick to "Lord Jesus Christ, Son of God, have mercy on me, a miserable sinner." Any formula that appeals to you will do. Within less than a month I noticed there was a marked change in my prayer.

All I did was repeat this aspiration of mine as often during the day as I remembered to, not only during the time of prayer but also at periods when I happened to be free: when I waited for a bus or train or was walking from one place to another. The change I experienced is hard to describe. It was nothing sensational. I began to feel more peaceful, more recollected, and more integrated, and, if it makes any sense, I began to feel a certain depth within me. I also noticed that the prayer had the habit of springing to my lips almost automatically any time I was not occupied with some mental activity. Then I would become aware of it and consciously repeat it, sometimes just mechanically, sometimes meaningfully.

I took this matter up with a sister I knew well, who had a good deal of experience in prayer and in spiritual direction. She had never read the book, but she told me of an interesting experience she herself had had. When she was a novice her novice mistress had told the novices to choose an aspiration that fitted into the rhythm of their walk. With the simple-heartedness characteristic of a novice, she took up this practice and kept repeating this formula mentally to the rhythm of her walk. Some time after the novitiate, she gave up the practice. However, the effects had lasted all her life. She said to me, "I don't know why it is, but each time I walk I am conscious that prayer is going on within me. I may be working at my desk when someone calls me to the parlor. The moment I stand up and begin to walk I become prayerful!" She attributed this to the practice of her Jesus Prayer when she was a novice. She also told me of a retreat master who said to a group of workers, "Set a prayer to the rhythm of the machines in your factory. Any prayer, like 'Sacred Heart of Jesus, I trust in Thee.' And keep repeating that prayer mentally all day in tune with the rhythm of the machines. It won't be long before you notice many spiritual benefits coming to you from this practice." The retreat master was right. The whole thing seems so mechanical, but it certainly seems to work. So I set out to do as much research as possible into the practice of this Jesus Prayer. There is much that I discovered, and I certainly don't plan to share with you here all I learned, only what might help you to practice it effectively yourselves.

I had initially been inclined to put down this practice to a species of autosuggestion. I'm not saying now that there aren't elements of autosuggestion here; there probably are. However, I was impressed by the vast number of theologians and saints who practiced and recommended this prayer in the past. These men and women may not have had all the refinement of psychological knowledge that we have today, but they were certainly not so naive as to be unable to distinguish a purely psychological phenomenon from a spiritual one. They frequently posed such problems to themselves and, it seems to me, answered them satisfactorily. I found that this practice was not limited only to the Eastern Churches. Many mystics of the Western Church practiced this prayer. The western formula was generally, "My Jesus, mercy." But there was a rich variety of formulas. We read of St. Francis of Assisi saying all night, *Deus meus et omnia.* (My God and my all.) St. Bruno, the founder of the Carthusians, was always saying *O bonitas!* (O goodness of God!) When St. Francis Xavier was dying off the coast of China, he was heard to be saying ceaselessly, "Lord Jesus Christ, Son of David, have mercy on me." St. Ignatius of Loyola in his Spiritual Exercises has a mysterious form of prayer that he recommends to a retreatant: to recite a prayer formula to the rhythm of one's breathing. I wonder where he discovered this equivalent of the Jesus Prayer.

It seems fairly certain that this practice in the Church originated from the Hindus in India who have an experience of six thousand years and more in the practice of the Prayer of the Name, as they call it. Incidentally, the Desert Fathers almost certainly practiced this form of prayer. The formula most commonly in use among them was the *Deus in adjutorium meum intende, Domine ad adjuvandum me festina.* (God come to my help. Lord, hasten to help me.) They would recite this formula all day during their hours of manual labor and most of the night when they kept their vigil. The reason why we know so little about their practice of this "opus," this "work" as they called it, is that they strictly followed the injunction that is common to a number of Hindu masters: Receive your formula from your guru or master and work at it all your life—and never reveal your formula to anyone except your master. To reveal the formula was to make it lose its power! So they were reticent about their use of the prayer.

How to Practice This Prayer

If you are interested in drawing the benefits from this form of prayer that the saints say it has, I advise you to choose some aspiration that appeals to you and recite it all through the day. There is no better time to get started on this prayer than the time of a retreat when you are not distracted with other concerns and occupations and can give a lot of time to letting this prayer "get into your blood," so to speak, and become a mental habit for you. That is the reason why I speak about it right at the start of the retreat. Strive to recite your formula mentally throughout the day—while eating, walking, bathing, even while listening to these talks and while meditating—unless it clearly distracts you. Let the words you have chosen ("Lord Jesus Christ, have mercy on me," or whatever your formula is) resound at the back of your mind while you listen to this conference or are praying or reflecting during your hours of meditation. Do not worry that the words seem to be repeated mechanically. I shall soon explain to you the value of what seems to be the mechanical recitation of a meaningless formula!

Traditionally your formula was supposed to be chosen for you by your spiritual guide, who was supposed to be experienced in the use of this prayer. Since I am, unfortunately, not expert enough in this prayer to be able to guide others, I suggest that you ask the Lord himself to guide you in the selection of a suitable formula. Whatever the formula you choose, nearly all the great masters, both Christian and non-Christian, insist that it contain some name of

God. The name of God is a sacramental and gives a special power to the prayer. The Eastern Christian masters give a great value to their own formula in its various forms, chiefly to the words *Jesus* and *mercy*. Incidentally, *mercy* does not mean just the pardon of sins, it stands for God's graciousness and loving kindness. However, as I said earlier, you may take any formula that appeals to you. "Sacred Heart of Jesus, I trust in Thee," is a favorite with many. Here are some others: "Lord Jesus Christ, thy kingdom come"; "My Lord and my God"; "My God and my all." You may also just take the name of Jesus. Just one word, recited repeatedly with different sentiments; love, adoration, praise, contrition. Other words for God— "God" or "Heart" or "Fire"—are recommended by the author of *The Cloud of Unknowing*, or you may prefer that precious cry of the Spirit within our hearts, that prayer that is most appropriate for a Christian, "Abba." I am told that the accent is on the second syllable in the Aramaic language; that gives it a nice sound, I think.

Whatever the formula you choose, it is a great help that it be three things: rhythmical, resonant, and uniform. (1) *Rhythmical.* I do not know why it is, but rhythm helps prayer to penetrate deep, right to the center of our being. Recite your prayer slowly, unhurriedly, and rhythmically, and it will be much more effective. (2) *Resonant.* This is not always possible, unfortunately, in English. Some of the Mediterranean languages, Spanish, Italian, are better for this. Latin is even better. Sanskrit is the very best I know of: it has formulas and names for God that have been developed over centuries. What can beat the sacred sound "om" for resonance and solemnity and depth? There are dozens of Sanskrit names for God and Sanskrit mantras. When they are chanted, they have the quality of just drawing you deeper into yourself and into God. Take the *Hari Om*, for instance or *Hare Ram, Ram Hare Hare.* If you find these formulas a help, I would have no hesitation in your using them and applying them to Our Lord Jesus Christ. All these names are his by right. He is the true Krishna, the true Vishnu, the true Rama. (3) *Uniform.* Once you have chosen a formula, don't change it easily. If you are constantly changing your formula it doesn't have a chance to get into your bloodstream, to become part of your unconscious self, as I shall explain later. I am not against your changing your formula if, after a period of trial, you find it doesn't suit you or you come across another that suits you better. If you have faith, sooner or later, through some trial and error, the Spirit will lead you to the formula that suits you best. The important thing is not to change it just because you are passing through a period of dryness and desolation. This is one of the common trials of the spiritual life and will occur no matter what form of prayer you adopt. To change one's style of prayer merely because one is attacked by a bout of dryness is indicative of superficiality. The dryness must come if the prayer is to sink deep into us. This is particularly true of the formulas we use for prayer—very much including the eucharistic prayers and prayers of the breviary. A time comes when the words become tasteless to our spiritual palate. They become meaningless; they dry up and begin to rot and decay, and we are tempted to reject them. However, if we patiently persevere in reciting our formulas, chiefly our Jesus Prayer, with whatever little devotion we can muster, the formulas will slowly spring to life again and take on an unsuspected depth and richness and give us delightful spiritual nourishment.

You can introduce a great deal of variety within the same formula (and variety seems to be needed especially for the apprentice in prayer) by giving different meanings to the same word. For instance, how many meanings can be put into the word *mercy*? We think of love, graciousness, pardon, peace, joy, comfort, strength—anything we desire from the Lord. You can recite the name of Jesus with different dispositions, making it a prayer of love or of adoration or of gratitude or whatever. Or you could introduce new words into the same formula, like this: "Jesus, I love you. Jesus, have mercy. Jesus, have pity. Jesus, remember me." Or, "Jesus, pity, Jesus, pity . . . Jesus, love, Jesus, love . . . Jesus, come, Jesus, come . . . Jesus, my God, Jesus, my God . . ." Your own inventiveness will suggest to you other ways of keeping the same formula but with a certain amount of variety. However, I must warn you that no matter how many efforts you may make at variety, you will have to budget for attacks of dryness and disgust, and persevere through these moods till the prayer finally triumphs and possesses your whole being.

Some masters recommend that in the early stages the prayer be recited aloud. I know of one great Hindu master whose whole being was possessed by the name of God, as he claims, as a result of his spending five hours each day on the banks of the river shouting out the Name in a loud voice. He did this when he was a young man; each day after he returned from work at his office, he would go to the riverbank to undertake his five hours of "spiritual work." There is no need really to recite your prayer aloud; mental recitation will do well enough. However, it is a help sometimes to recite it in a loud or a low voice when you are alone. This way your tongue, your mind, your heart, your whole being will be disciplined and molded into the Divine Name and it will become indelibly engraved in your being.

One last word, this one of caution, with regard to the practice of the Prayer of the Name. If you ever read any literature on this subject, you may learn there of some psychophysiological techniques for "putting the prayer into the heart." My advice to you is that you steer clear of all these techniques. They may awaken within you forces from the unconscious that you are not able to control. Go in for these techniques (if at all) only under the expert guidance of an experienced and trustworthy master. This is especially true of techniques that involve forms of forced concentration and of breath control.

The Power of the Prayer of the Name

There is an endless amount of Hindu literature on this subject that is very inspirational because it comes from people who have

experienced the marvelous effects of this prayer in their lives. Here
are some samples of what the Hindu masters write:

I am particularly impressed by the words of Mahatma Gandhi,
that spiritual giant who lived out his life of prayer in the midst of
the world of politics and reform and revolution. He was in the
habit of reciting the Hindu name of God, *Rama*. He called it his
Ramanama (name of Rama).

> As a child, there was in me a fear of ghosts and spirits. Rambha,
> my nurse, suggested, as a remedy for this fear, the repetition of
> Ramanama. I had more faith in her than in her remedy, and so
> at a tender age I began repeating Ramanama to cure my fear of
> ghosts and spirits. . . . I think it is due to the seed sown by that
> good woman Rambha that today Ramanama has become an
> infallible remedy for me. Our most powerful ally in conquer-
> ing animal passion is Ramanama or some similar mantra. . . .
> One must be completely absorbed in whatever mantra one se-
> lects. . . . The mantra becomes one's staff of life and carries one
> through every ordeal. . . . Ramanama gives one detachment
> and ballast, and never throws one off at critical moments. . . .
> The latter part of the second fast went fairly hard with me. I
> had not then completely understood the wonderful efficacy of
> Ramanama, and my capacity for suffering was to that extent
> less. . . . Ramanama is a sun that has brightened my darkest
> hour. A Christian may find the same solace from the repetition
> of the name of Jesus and a Muslim from the name of Allah. . . .
> No matter what the ailment from which a man may be suffer-
> ing, recitation of Ramanama from the heart is the sure cure.
> God has many names. Each person can choose the name that
> appeals most to him. . . . Ramanama cannot perform the mira-
> cle of restoring to you a lost limb. But it can perform the still
> greater miracle of helping you to enjoy an ineffable peace in
> spite of the loss while you live, and rob death of its sting and
> the grave of its victory at the journey's end. . . . There is no

doubt that Ramanama is the surest aid. If recited from the heart, it charms away every evil thought, and evil thought gone, no corresponding action is possible. . . . I can say fearlessly that there is no connection between Ramanama of my conception and jantar mantar (the repetition of superstitious and magical formulas). I have said that to recite Ramanama from the heart means deriving help from an incomparable power. The atom bomb is as nothing compared with it. This power is capable of removing all pain.

Gandhi was a firm believer in the power of the Name even to the extent of believing that it alone could cure one of physical illnesses. He called it "the poor man's medicine" and even went to the extent of saying that he would never die of any illness. If he did, the world could write the word *hypocrite* as his epitaph. A few months before he died at the age of seventy-eight, he was making a vigorous pilgrimage through the riot-striken areas of Bengal, barefoot. Occasionally, he would have violent attacks of dysentery, but he always refused to accept medicine for it, claiming that the recitation of God's name would pull him through. It always seemed to do so, and he enjoyed good health until the day he was assassinated.

The use of the Prayer of the Name by an active politician like Gandhi is particularly reassuring to those who would like to give this prayer a try but are afraid that it is a form of prayer more suited to the monastic than to the active life. I know many, many men and women who lead very active lives and who have found, through the use of this prayer, a wonderful means of keeping united with God constantly. I am reminded particularly of a sister who was a physician and was having trouble keeping united with God throughout the day. She put the problem to me well: "I give all my thoughts to my patients. Frequently, while walking through the wards of the hospital I get a sudden insight into the nature and the cure of someone's illness. This would not happen if I were constantly thinking of God. And yet, I would like to be aware of God all through the day. I suppose that that just isn't my vocation." She was confusing prayer with thought, as so many people do. You don't always need your mind to pray. In fact, the mind is frequently a positive obstacle to prayer, as I shall show you some time later in this retreat. You pray with your heart not with your mind, just as you listen to music with your ear and smell a rose with your nose. This sister was obviously right in giving all her thoughts to her patients. That is just what God wanted of her. I suggested that she try the Jesus Prayer. She was considerably skeptical at first. Six months later I happened to meet her and she told me she was having much less of a problem (frequently no problem at all) with regard to being aware of God's loving presence and being united with him while simultaneously giving her thoughts to the problems of her patients. The nearest comparison I can think of is that of listening to background music, being dimly and pleasantly aware of it, while giving all my attention to a conversation with a friend or to reading the newspaper.

The Power in Jesus' Name

The New Testament gives us clear indications of the value and the power of Jesus' name, a name that is more potent than all the names of God revealed to humankind.

> Therefore God raised him to the heights and bestowed on him the name above all other names, that at the name of Jesus every knee should bow—in heaven, on earth, and in the depths—and every tongue confess, 'Jesus Christ is Lord', to the glory of God the Father.
>
> Philippians 2:9–11

> There is no salvation in anyone else at all, for there is no other name under heaven granted to men, by which we may receive salvation.
>
> Acts 4:12

In very truth I tell you, if you ask the Father for anything in
my name, he will give it you. So far you have asked nothing in
my name. Ask and you will receive, that your joy may be
complete.

John 16:23–24

We read in Exodus 20:7, "You shall not take the name of the
Lord your God in vain; for the Lord will not hold him guiltless
who takes his name in vain." God protects his own name from
being used unworthily just as he protects life and honor and prop-
erty. In nearly all ancient religions there is the belief that whoever
had the Divine Name had also the power contained in that name.
For the name was not an empty sound. It not merely signified the
God whom it pointed to; it frequently carried with it the power
and the grace and the presence of this God. This is what dozens of
Catholic contemplatives have felt instinctively with regard to the
mightiest name of God known to humankind, the name of Jesus.
Let us recite it frequently, with love and devotion, with faith and
tenderness, with adoration and reverence, and it will not be long
before we confirm with our own experience the wisdom of these
great contemplatives.

The "Psychological" Reasons
behind This Prayer

By way of an appendix to the Prayer of the Name I should like
to add something about the psychology of this form of prayer. I do
this because I am frequently confronted with the difficulties of retreatants who would like to use this form of prayer but draw back
because they consider it too mechanical, too parrot-like—an "act
of man," not a "human act" was the way one priest put it to me,
using terms that we were familiar with from our training in moral
theology. If you find what I am going to say now a distraction, for-

get all about it and embark upon the practice of the prayer in faith and simplicity.

Some years ago I became familiar with the works of a Frenchman named Emile Coue who reported extraordinary healings through his technique of what he called autosuggestion. I am going to explain to you now how autosuggestion is said to work and speak about the unconscious and its power over us. You will have to be patient because I shall apply all this psychological theory to the Jesus Prayer right at the end, and I trust that your patience will then be rewarded.

Let's begin with the unconscious. This is a notion popularized by Freud, who claimed that the unconscious is the major part of the human personality. It is like the part of the iceberg that is submerged under the sea. The small part of that mighty mountain of ice that juts out of the ocean is similar to the conscious mind and will of human beings. The unconscious is a much more important factor of our personality; it is the seat of all our hidden drives and urges and passions and instincts.

To prove the existence of the unconscious Freud had recourse to dreams and hypnotism. Let's limit ourselves to the phenomenon of hypnotism. Let's suppose I hypnotize John and while he is under the hypnotic trance I make a suggestion to him. I say to him, "Tomorrow, at 10 a.m. you will take this book from the library and give it to Henry." I then bring John out of the trance. He has no memory of what I said to him when he was in the trance. The next day, a little after 10 o'clock, I find John moving away from the library in the direction of Henry's room. I stop him and ask where he is going. "To Henry," he says, "to give him this book." "Why?" I ask. "Because," says John, "there's a chapter on prayer in this book that I am sure will interest Henry." "Are you sure that is the reason why you want to give that book to Henry?" I ask, incredulously. "Of course," says John, "what other reason is there?" It is now his turn to be incredulous! We know, of course that the "conscious" motive for John's giving the book to Henry is that chapter on prayer. That is the motive John is aware of. But we also know that there is a deeper motive pushing John towards Henry's room with that book in his hand—an "unconscious" motive of which he is not aware. This is, of course, a somewhat frightening matter. If John feels consciously free in this activity and is, in reality, not quite as free as he thinks he is, how are we to know whether he is really free in so much of his other activity? How much of it is really controlled by motives and conditioning that he is simply not aware of? That is a problem for theologians and psychologists to grapple with. While the discovery of the unconscious brings its problems with it, it also reveals to us an immense reservoir of power that is largely untapped.

I read of an incident that took place in the U.S. some years ago. An elderly woman was caught under a huge truck and it was impossible to move her without lifting the truck. The truck was too heavy for human hands to lift; so while everyone was waiting for the arrival of a crane, a small man passed by on the other side, saw the woman under the truck, and instinctively went up to the truck, caught the fender with both hands, and lifted the truck effortlessly while the bystanders extricated the woman! When the newspapers heard of this fact, the man was besieged by reporters who wanted him to repeat the performance so that they could photograph it. But, try as he might, he just couldn't. What had happened? In a crisis, he suddenly drew upon the tremendous resources of power that were lying untapped within him. He was convinced he could move the truck—so he moved it. I have read of similar feats performed by Hindu saints who would fast for days on end and then undertake difficult physical tasks like climbing mountains or walking long distances. I tend to believe this and to believe also, that there are immense reservoirs of power within us of which we know nothing; that there is a whole universe waiting to be explored within us, inner space, to which, unfortunately, we give little attention, while we direct all our efforts to the conquest of the outer world and outer space.

To return to hypnotism. It would seem that if you could convince the unconscious of something, that something is likely to come true in you. The unconscious seems to be wide open to suggestion while you are in the hypnotic trance. Here's another example: The hypnotist says to his subject, "Would you like a cigarette?" Then instead of a cigarette, he offers him a stick of chalk which the subject immediately proceeds to "smoke" and enjoy! Then, suddenly, the hypnotist says, "Look, you've burned your finger!" The startled subject immediately flings the "cigarette" away, and, right enough, a physical burn begins to form on his finger, with the accompanying destruction of flesh tissue! What is this enormous power of suggestion that we have within us? Is there some means of sanctifying this unconscious? Most of our spirituality seems to be geared to the conscious mind. What about the hidden part of the iceberg? To sanctify that would be to sanctify our motivation and activity and the sources of much of our power at their roots. Is there some way of getting in touch with this unconscious, of influencing it and of using it to our benefit?

Emile Coue claimed there was. He called it autosuggestion. Briefly, this was his theory: Through autosuggestion it is possible to cure almost any disease and to bring health and vigor to your body. All you need do is convince your unconscious you are healthy. How? Let's suppose you have an ulcer of the stomach. Then, each night before you go to sleep (that seems to be the time when the unconscious is wide open to suggestion) you must lie relaxedly in bed and say, slowly, about twenty times, the following formula, "Every day, in every way, I am getting better and better." According to Coue, it won't be long before the unconscious gets the message and your ulcer disappears! If you are to influence the unconscious, however, there are two important things you must avoid. The first is thinking of your ulcer explicitly while you recite the formula. If you do this the unconscious will somehow resist this direct attempt on your part to influence it. You must not think of your ulcer. Think of health in general. The ulcer will go on its own. The second thing to avoid is concentrating on the meaning of the words you are saying. Once again this would be an attempt at direct influence. The unconscious "knows" the meaning of those words; so don't you emphasize it with your conscious mind. Think, rather, of health in a general way.

Isn't this exactly what happens in the Jesus Prayer? We recite those words frequently during the day without adverting directly to the meaning of the words. This, far from being a loss, may be an actual gain. There is an awareness that the words are words of prayer, that prayer is going on. Gradually, the unconscious catches on and becomes, for lack of a better word, "prayerful." You begin to notice, after a while, that all your life and activity is being invaded by this prayerfulness. So even though, at first sight, this form of prayer may seem to be what my priest called an "act of man" rather than a "human act," because the conscious mind and will is not directly engaged in it, it is as human and effective an act as is the act of influencing the unconscious through autosuggestion.

Some people find it repugnant to think that the laws of autosuggestion may be operating in the Jesus Prayer. But why should they not? Why may we not use the power of autosuggestion to become more prayerful and come nearer to God just as we use the force of our mind and imagination and emotion?

The Rosary

Some of you may have noticed how everything I have said about the Jesus Prayer applies perfectly to the recitation of the rosary. It is fashionable nowadays to deride this practice of repetitious prayer. If you examine the rosary with your "rational" mind, there is every reason to believe that it is not a prayer, only a parody of prayer. The same formula, the Hail Mary, is repeated

again and again, monotonously, impersonally, without our adverting to the meaning of the words—in fact, we are even encouraged
not to think about the meaning, we are encouraged not to indulge
in a pious distraction, so to speak, by meditating on the life of
Christ with our minds while saying "Hail Mary, full of grace . . ."
with our mouths. "Prayer wheel" has been the reaction of some
people. Would it not be much better to make some spontaneous
prayer to the Lord? I know of one priest who, to show a group of
women the ridiculousness of the rosary, began his talk to them
with "Good morning, ladies!" They replied, "Good morning, Father!" "Good morning, ladies!" said the priest again, and again and
again. Then he stopped and said, "You probably think I've gone
mad! That's what Mary probably thinks of us when we keep saying the Hail Mary again and again." A good argument indeed. But
the trouble with the deep things of the spirit is that they are not
quite subject to human logic and human reason. There are deeper
things in life than human reason is able to grasp. The human mind
can give us cleverness, not wisdom. For this, one needs a sense, an
instinct that is beyond the mind. This is the instinct the saints had
when they practiced and recommended this form of prayer. One
reads of great contemplatives, like the Jesuit lay brother, St.
Alphonsus Rodriguez, who would recite dozens of rosaries each
day. One meets some holy old women in our Indian villages
whose faces are lined with suffering and love and are radiant with
the quiet glow of the Spirit; their only prayer is the recitation of
the rosary. All the principles of the Jesus Prayer apply here. Here
once again we have what I like to call the sanctification of the unconscious through the seemingly mechanical recitation of a prayer
formula.

If the rosary has appealed to you in the past, make that your
Jesus Prayer. Or use your beads while reciting your own prayer formula. I don't know why it is, but the fingering of the beads brings
to many people peace and prayerfulness; it is probably because it
brings rhythm into the prayer. I sometimes pass my beads through

my fingers without saying any prayer; and the gesture alone is enough to put me into prayer. Do something like this at your prayer today. Use your beads to recite your Jesus Prayer rhythmically. And with the blessing of the Blessed Virgin, may you discover the wisdom that so many saints found in prayer.

9

Shared Prayer

I am going to talk to you about a form of prayer that, on the face of it, would seem to have no place in the kind of retreat I am offering you. At least, so I thought for many years. For years I was much opposed to what has now-a-days come to be known as shared prayer. Shared prayer might have a place in "group" retreats where retreatants sought an experience of Christ in community. This is a "desert" retreat, one where the retreatant seeks Christ in strict silence and solitude and confrontation with him- or herself. All communication, group discussions, sharing sessions, even communication in prayer, was, I felt, a distraction. I still maintain most of this. A group retreat offers the retreatant what an individual retreat does not, and vice versa. I strongly recommend that every priest have an experience of both kinds of retreat; they complement each other. But I am opposed to mixing the two. When this is done they get in each other's way, and the effect is watered down. If you are making a silent retreat, plunge as deeply as possible into silence, avoid all talk and discussions like the plague, otherwise you are constantly knocking down with one hand what you are building up with the other. A group retreat has techniques and methods all its own, and group interaction there, far from being an obstacle to meeting Christ, is actually a means by which we encounter him.

I also had personal reasons against shared prayer. It just didn't fit into the religious culture in which I had grown, so I found excellent reasons against it. It was like making love in public, I said. Moreover, after a while a person is able to communicate with God beyond all words and concepts. How does one share that kind of prayer with a group? All one would say is something like "My God, I love you," a very trite thing to say: full of meaning for me, but hardly likely to thrill or inspire the other members of the group. These prejudices of mine have ceased, I am happy to say. I have discovered that there is a form of prayer one uses with God when one is alone with him, and a form of prayer that one can share—to one's own spiritual benefit and that of others. Let me tell you how I discovered the value of shared prayer.

I was once giving a thirty-day retreat to a group of Jesuits. Towards the middle of the retreat I thought of all I had been reading at that time about the Catholic pentecostal movement (or charismatic renewal movement as it is called now). How generous the Lord seemed to be in pouring the gifts of his Spirit into these Catholics who sought him in fervor and simplicity. And they weren't making thirty-day retreats! So I said to the retreatants, If God is being so generous with these people, he is surely going to be very generous with you who are seeking him so earnestly over a period of a whole month in prayer and silence. If we feel he is not being generous enough it is probably because we don't pray to him enough as a group. I therefore suggested that from that night onward we have exposition of the Blessed Sacrament and adoration at night before retiring to sleep. The retreatants were free to come or not; if they came, however, they were to come to pray, not for themselves, but for the whole group, to pray earnestly that the whole group would receive a fresh infusion of the Holy Spirit.

Everyone came. The atmosphere in the chapel was most conducive to prayer, with the lights out and the host standing out in the darkness, lit up by the candles in front of the monstrance. We prayed for each other in silence. And it wasn't long before I sensed a marked increase in the graces the retreatants were receiving. They noticed it too. However, the skeptic in me hesitated to attribute this to the night intercession. Could it not be that the previous two weeks of silence had disposed the retreatants to receive these graces, so that they would have received them whether we had had our group intercession or not? I continued to recommend this practice to retreatants at eight-day retreats. This time I could not doubt the effects. There was a marked difference between these retreats and the ones I had given before. The conferences were the same, the techniques, the methods of prayer, were all the same, but the graces that God was pouring out on these retreats were definitely greater than the graces he seemed to be giving in former retreats. It was hard to avoid the conclusion that it was the group prayer at night that was making the difference.

Then a retreatment came to me and said, "Would it be all right for us to pray aloud? It is easier to pray for people whose needs we know than to just pray for the group in general." I agreed reluctantly because of the reservation I had with regard to shared prayer. I am very glad I agreed. Some of the retreatants would ask for specific graces. They would either address the Lord ("Lord, give me the grace to pray. I keep trying all day and don't seem to succeed. I'm just overwhelmed with distractions.") or their fellow retreatants ("Brothers, I ask you to pray that I will be given the grace of repentance. Somehow I seem to have lost the sense of sin and the sense of my need of God"). Again and again these persons who had had the courage to ask for some grace aloud would report that they were given these graces thanks to the prayers of the whole group. It was a literal fulfillment of Jesus' words,

> I tell you this: if two of you agree on earth about any request you have to make, that request will be granted by my Heavenly Father. For where two or three have met together in my name, I am there among them.
>
> Matthew 18:19–20

So in the beginning this was the simple form of shared prayer we practiced. If you wanted some grace, you mentioned it at our group prayer, and we would all pray for you, generally in silence. When God gave you the grace you had asked for, you came to give thanks publicly at our prayer session, so that we would all join in praising and thanking him and he would receive greater glory and love for his goodness toward you. I now began to recommend this form of shared prayer to all my retreatants right from the first day of the retreat and saw again and again how quickly they attained the graces they were seeking, something I was not accustomed to seeing in my retreats in the past.

Then I began to discover the value of shared prayer in areas outside the retreat. What a difference it would make to a group discussion, to a consultation, to a decision-making session, if we would stop to pray, not just at the beginning and the end of the session, but at times when we are stuck or are making no headway or are in need of light and guidance or are all worked up and angry and quarrelsome and defensive. I saw these prayer sessions do wonders in bringing people together, in uniting communities, in bridging the generation gap, where other methods (community dialogue, encounter groups, etc.) had failed. I see now, sadly, that we priests rarely pray together in other than the somewhat stylized forms prescribed by the liturgy. Our meetings and discussions, especially the meetings of our decision-making bodies, are rarely different from a meeting of executives of a secular firm: there's a good deal of horse sense and human prudence and, hopefully, good surveys and plenty of information relating to the problems to be discussed, but little direct communication with God and reliance on his inspiration and guidance.

This was well expressed by an American priest, Rev. Joseph M. O'Meara, in an article entitled "Contrasting Conventions: Prayer Makes a Difference."

During this past month I attended two conventions, one in Baltimore and one in Washington. Both were about religion. But what a difference!

The first was the annual convention of the National Federation of Priests' Councils, the second the annual convention of the Full Gospel Business Men's Fellowship International. The Fellowship is an organization of Christian, Protestant denominational, nondenominational, Catholic, even Jewish people, who have reached out for a deep experience with the Lord Jesus and found the conventional methods of evangelism wanting. It is basically Pentecostal or charismatic in nature. . . .

The Fellowship, which began as recently as 1953 here in the U.S., has over five hundred chapters in this country and many chapters in other countries. They have reached a point where they now add a chapter a day to their fellowship. While we lose scores of priests almost daily, they gain scores of ministers for the Lord daily. While our church members are becoming rapidly disillusioned with the effectiveness of Christianity, their members are enthusiastically speaking of the wondrous effectiveness of the Lord within themselves and throughout the world. While our members grow even more reluctant to speak of any personal relationship or experience with the Lord, their members are eager to tell what the Lord has done for them and with their lives.

I heard a young man, twenty-three years old, tell how this personal experience of the Lord has reversed his drug-centered and LSD-centered life to a life of love and dedication for Jesus. There are many such testimonies of young people under the influence of the Fellowship. How many of us can go into our churches and find such fruit? I listened to a Jewish man tell how he was about to become a eunuch for the Lord; a man, though married, living as though unmarried because his apostolate was making such demands upon him. What a stark contrast to the proceedings of the NFPC on a related point!

Why is all this happening with them and not with us and other Christian churches? I don't know the whole answer, but I do know it in part. Prayer! That's the part I know!

These people at the Fellowship convention didn't discuss a person, place or thing that they didn't pray over it, under it, beside it, for it, with it and during it. Prayer in song and word was on their lips constantly. At the NFPC convention there was hardly a prayer uttered.

Between sessions the Fellowship were gathered together in rooms praying together and relating their personal experiences of the Lord and how they were going to spread His wonderful Word. Between sessions at the NFPC we were gathered together in rooms sipping cocktails and discussing Church politics. At the Fellowship nothing was undertaken without calling upon the Holy Spirit to guide it. At the NFPC convention we seemed to proceed all too much like natural men.

I have learned that a shared prayer session is not the distraction that a group discussion can be to a silent retreat; provided, of course there isn't more than one session a day, else there is the danger of the retreatants taking refuge in this, relatively more comfortable, form of prayer to escape the rigors of a personal encounter with God. The group discussion, unlike the shared prayer, is likely to arouse emotions that need to be worked through afterward and can be a real disturbance to the interior silence that the retreat gives you. There was something else. I found that shared prayer gave some of the retreatants the advantages of prophecy! More than once retreatants have told me that a prayer they heard in the session, a reflection that was made there, an insight that was shared made a tremendous difference to their retreat. It was as if the Lord himself was speaking to them through the person who was sharing or praying (and that is what the gift of prophecy is, the Lord speaking to me through my brother, even though he is not aware of it). I found it interesting to see how often prophecy was exercised in the form of prayers, rather than insights or sermons, frequently prayers that, on the surface, seemed quite ordinary. Someone would say a simple prayer and one or two or more of the others would be plunged into a mood of devotion or given the light and inspiration they needed.

How to Go about It

There are no rules for shared prayer. But I think it will help if I list some of the difficulties that shared prayer runs into and some of the things that help it to be fruitful. Here, are some of the difficulties:

1. Going to a session to do your own private prayer. If you do this, you are likely to find the talking a distraction and you may be something of a silent burden to the group. Not that silence is an obstacle to shared prayer, quite the contrary, as I shall soon say. But you are just not with the others in spirit, and so you will be something of a disturbance to them as they will be to you. Retreatants have sometimes told me that they get nothing out of shared prayer. This has sometimes happened because they went to the session to continue with their personal form of prayer, the Jesus Prayer or the Prayer of Faith or whatever. Shared prayer requires that you take up another form of praying, another disposition. You go there to pray with others, to pray for them and to ask for their prayers, to be open to what they are saying to you and to what the Spirit may inspire you to say to them. When you take up this attitude shared prayer becomes very profitable and fruitful, even when most of it is done in silence.

2. Too much "cerebration." It is important that the shared prayer be not glutted with thoughts, reflections, and insights. There is a place for these, of course. But most people find it easier to share their ideas than to share their prayer. Ordinarily, when someone is praying to the Lord, our heart is more easily touched by grace than when someone is talking to us about some insight received in prayer.

Beware of that form of sharing insights by which we are really talking to the members of the group, but we add the word "Lord" to what we are saying. It is more forthright, and less distracting, to say, "Friends, here's an insight or a reflection I want to share with you . . ." than to say, "Lord . . ." and then proceed to lecture us. Here is a good example of what I mean: "Lord, you know how much harm is being done to the Church by the so-called liberals and scripture scholars. In my opinion, Lord, they are the cause of all the turmoil in the Church today . . ." This is an example of how, unfortunately, under cover of speaking to the Lord, we can even have digs at one another!

3. The third difficulty I would list here could be called "impersonality." The use of the pronoun *we*, instead of *I*. "Lord, we thank you for your goodness to us." Don't speak for the rest of us. Leave that to the celebrant who presides over the liturgy. Don't take it upon yourself to interpret the sentiments and feelings of the rest of the group. Speak for yourself. Your prayer will be much more personal. You are sharing nothing when you say "we"; you have merely made yourself our spokesperson.

4. A more serious difficulty is not listening to one another. For example, Jim makes an anguished prayer to the Lord, calling out to him for help in despair, and then, barely a second after the prayer has ended, Tom pipes in on a cheerful note to thank the Lord for some favor or other. Wasn't Tom listening to Jim? It seems almost indecent to rush in with a joyful prayer without giving the rest of us at least a little while to be with Jim in his anguish and to pray for him. This is one of the reasons why it is a great help for the group to have a leader—one who doesn't stand out in the group, precisely, but who is attuned to what is going on within the group, listening both to the group members and to the Lord. In a situation like the one I have described, Jim may get the feeling that no one cares; if no one refers to his prayer explicitly, the leader may make a brief prayer for him aloud. This will be supportive and reassuring to those who have asked for help; their prayers have not been heard by the others with cold indifference. It is significant that when Jesus

was in agony he shared his prayer of anguish with his disciples. He allowed them to listen to what he was saying to his Father and looked for some support and comfort from them. If we do not listen to one another, then we are just not sharing in the prayer of one another.

Listening to the other's prayer implies that the other prays in an audible voice. It is very distracting, sometimes even irritating, when someone mumbles something that we have to strain our ears to catch. Speak up, or do not speak at all.

5. The next difficulty is not listening to the Lord who is speaking within our hearts. We can sometimes get so carried away by the prayers and problems of one another that the Lord is pushed into the background. We give him little scope for inspiring us, for speaking within our hearts, because we are too full of what we and others are saying to him.

And the Lord does speak to us very frequently. If we create an inner silence within ourselves we might sense him impelling us to utter a prayer or share some insight he is giving us. Through this prayer or insight of ours the Lord frequently activates the charism of prophecy within the group. Prophecy means speaking to someone on behalf of the Lord, giving someone a message from the Lord. This was a gift that was frequently exercised in the early Church. Paul valued it highly and urged his Christians to positively seek it because it helps so much for the spiritual growth of our neighbor (1 Corinthians 14). We find an outstanding example of prophecy in Acts 21.

> When we had been in Caesarea several days, a prophet named Agabus arrived from Judaea. He came to us, took Paul's belt, bound his own feet and hands with it, and said, "These are the words of the Holy Spirit: Thus will the Jews in Jerusalem bind the man to whom this belt belongs, and hand him over to the Gentiles." When we heard this, we and the local people begged and implored Paul to abandon his visit to Jerusalem.

I have sometimes witnessed this gift of prophecy in action. Nothing as sensational as the example of Agabus. Someone in the group would share an insight, be moved to read a passage from Scripture chosen at random, or would just make a simple prayer to the Lord, and someone else would feel the Lord speaking while the other was talking. So I urge people not to hold back whatever the Lord seems to be urging them to say, because he frequently gives to us what he means us to share with the others in the group. Hence it is important to be attentive to the Lord who may be speaking either in the silence of our hearts or in the words of others.

For this purpose it will be a help if the group leader suggests a period of silence prayer (a "listening session" some call it) whenever he or she notices that there is too much talking that doesn't seem charged with the spirit and unction of prayer. There will be times when the group will spontaneously lapse into silence. Silence is of two types. There is the dull, heavy silence in which we get a sense that nothing is happening, and we're grounded. When there is too much of this, I suggest that the members stop the prayer for a while and search for the cause of this deadness: are they being too sluggish or too inhibited? Are they really comfortable with the silence? Generally this sluggishness and deadness is dispelled through singing some hymns, chiefly hymns of praise and thanksgiving, and the reading of a passage or two from Scripture.

There is another type of silence when the whole atmosphere is obviously charged with prayerfulness. It is full of unction; everyone is clearly steeped in prayer. This is beautiful, and it is a grave mistake to break in with a prayer or a hymn just so that "things will start moving." It requires some spiritual sensitiveness to distinguish one silence from the other, and here, too, the leader can be of help.

6. Here's another difficulty: long-winded prayers and what I call "praying to the gallery." It is important that prayers be not too long. After a while, it becomes difficult to be attentive to what the

prayer is saying. Better to pray ten times in a prayer session for half a minute or a minute each time than inflict a lengthy prayer of five or six minutes' duration on us.

Praying to the gallery is an attempt to impress people with our prayer. We sometimes carefully rehearse our prayers before we launch out, either because we are nervous or because we want to impress. The ideal prayers are those made with our eyes fixed on the Lord to whom we are praying without too much care for grammar and sentence structure. These prayers are simple and spontaneous and the bad grammar doesn't disturb. We cannot, of course, be entirely unmindful of the presence of others and pray to the Lord as though they were not there. Only let's make sure that it is to him that we are addressing our words, that it is for his ears our prayers are composed, not for those of the group.

7. The final difficulty I want to list here is coming to the prayer meeting without having spent some time previously in personal prayer. Shared prayer seems to be most fruitful when everyone participating in it has spent a good deal of time that day in private, personal prayer. I know of a charismatic renewal prayer group where there is an understanding that on the day of the prayer meeting, which is held at night, everyone pray for at least two whole hours. I was edified to learn that these people, laypersons most of them, would wake early in the morning, before setting out to work, to do scripture reading and to expose themselves to the presence of the Lord for the required two hours. It is no wonder to me that those prayer sessions were charged with the grace and unction of the Spirit. These people came to the meeting already charged with the spirit of prayer, not seeking to have their dead spiritual batteries recharged! This is probably the reason why shared prayer seems so much more fruitful during a retreat when everyone is investing much time in personal prayer.

Further Tips on How to Go about It

Ideally, shared prayer is unstructured, leaving the maximum freedom to people to intervene as the Spirit moves them. Someone may read a scripture passage, another sing a hymn (with the others joining in or not as they feel moved to do so), and yet another share a reflection or make a prayer. There is no fixed order.

However, it helps to begin with a brief period of silence during which participants can revive their faith in the presence of the Lord. This makes him present. A couple of hymns at the beginning are also a great help.

During the retreat the main emphasis in our shared prayer is asking the Lord for personal favors connected with the retreat and thanking him for giving them to us. Outside the retreat, we often practice the prayer of intercession—praying for the needs of others. Above all it helps to spend some time in the prayer of praise. When we praise God for his goodness and for the good things he has given to us and to others, our hearts become lightsome and joyous. It was only after I got acquainted with the charismatic renewal movement that I, myself, discovered the prayer of praise and its value. There are few forms of prayer so effective for giving you the sense that you are loved by God, or for lifting depressed spirits and overcoming temptation. Psalm 8 says, "You have established praise to destroy the enemy and avenger," and it was the custom among the Jews to march out into battle singing praises to the Lord. This was considered a mighty weapon for defeating the foe. We read in 2 Chronicles 20:21–22:

> Josaphat, as they set out, came forward to speak. Listen to me, he said, men of Juda; Listen, citizens of Jerusalem. Trust in the Lord your God, and you have nothing to fear; trust his prophets, and all shall go well with you. Thus he encouraged them, and would have the Lord's minstrels praise him in chorus, marching before the army and singing: Praise the Lord,

the Lord is gracious; his mercy endures for ever. As the chant rose, the Lord turned the stealthy approach of Juda's enemies, Ammon and Moab and Edom, to their own discomfiture.

In the Old Testament, incidentally, the prayer of praise was said aloud—you either shouted your praise or sang your praise. I have even had people tell me that they feel physically revived through practicing the prayer of praise. One laborer told me how, under cover of the din of his factory machines, he would spend a good part of his day praising God aloud (though not *too* loud for fear of being overheard by his companions), and he said it gave him the same invigorating effect after his night shift that he got from a cold shower and a hot cup of coffee.

When group prayer tends to grow heavy and to drag, the leader may say a few words about the prayer of praise and encourage everyone to fix their eyes on the Lord and praise him for everything, for things good and bad and, above all, for his being the good God that he is. This may be done either individually in the form of prayer or collectively with everyone singing a hymn of praise and thanksgiving and adoration. A marked change will soon come over the group.

One last and important suggestion for your shared prayer sessions, if you ever have them outside the retreat: fix the duration of the session before hand and let everyone know clearly how long it is going to last—half an hour, one hour, or two hours. Then when the time is up, even though most people feel inspired to continue, call a halt to the prayer to allow those who wish to leave to depart. The rest may then continue if you wish. This will spare many people the distraction and strain of constantly wondering when it is going to end!

Shared Prayer for the Priest

A priest is a spiritual leader and he will find a rich apostolate in the prayer group. I know a number of priests who, after experiencing the benefits of shared prayer in a retreat like this one, have begun to pray together with their lay collaborators, with their catechists and school staff—and gained much fruit thereby. We frequently visit our people, we call on sick people in hospitals, we offer counseling and spiritual direction to people in our offices. How rarely do we think of praying with these people. It just isn't in our tradition, as it is in the tradition of some Protestant pastors. It is more within our tradition to give the client or patient our blessing. I have sometimes ventured to pray with a client after a counseling session; both of us pray to the Lord who is present there with us, telling him of our hopes and disappointments and confusions and asking for his help. I have often found this part of the interview to be the most effective and healing for the client and for me!

Once we summon up the courage to pray, either before or after the interview (or even in the confessional) it becomes easier, and I haven't met one client who isn't glad to have me say a prayer with and for him or her. I am reminded here of what a woman, a former Catholic turned Pentecostal, said while in the hospital. "When my minister comes to visit me, he spends nearly half an hour praying and reading the Bible with me; that's what I want a minister for. When the Catholic priest visits me, he talks of politics and the weather, then gives me his blessing and goes away." It just isn't in our tradition, is it, to pray with a patient before we leave, or to say to a family we are visiting, "Shall I pray with you now before I leave?"

I have had quite some success getting families to join in shared prayer when I visit them. What I do is this: I begin to pray myself and then ask the others present if there is anything they want to say to the Lord. They always have a great deal to say to him. In the beginning they tell me, and I say the prayer to the Lord for them. In the later stages I get them to tell him themselves! Or I start with the rosary, a prayer that many families are already familiar with. Between decades I say, "Whom shall we offer this decade for?" Then I make a spontaneous prayer for all the people mentioned; gradu-

ally the others have no difficulty making this kind of prayer themselves.

In some retreats, when the number of retreatants is large, I invite the retreatants to split up into groups of ten to twelve for
shared prayer. Generally, as in this retreat, we have our shared
prayer before the Blessed Sacrament exposed, at night. I think for
most of you who come to this prayer, shared prayer will be an experience you will carry with you and treasure long after your retreat is over.

10

Repentance

It is customary, at the start of a retreat, to meditate on one's sinfulness, and to seek pardon of God through the grace of repentance. I wish to speak on this today: the theme of repentance.

Repentance: A Way to Experience Christ

Even though the experience of Christ is a grace we can never merit, I have already suggested two things we can do, two dispositions we can cultivate to prepare ourselves to receive this grace. These two things are the ardent desire to meet him and constant petitionary prayer. The third thing is repentance. This is splendidly put in the Book of Revelation:

> To the angel of the church at Ephesus write: "These are the words of the One who holds the seven stars in his right hand and walks among the seven lamps of gold; I know all your ways, your toil and your fortitude. I know you cannot endure evil men; you have put to the proof those who claim to be apostles but are not, and have found them false. Fortitude you have; you have borne up in my cause and never flagged. But I have this against you: you have lost your early love. Think from what a height you have fallen; repent and do as you once

did. Otherwise, if you do not repent, I shall come to you and remove your lamp from its place."

Revelation 2:1–5

To the angel of the Church at Laodicea write: "These are the words of the Amen, the faithful and true witness, the prime source of all God's creation: I know all your ways; you are neither hot nor cold. How I wish you were either hot or cold! But because you are lukewarm, neither hot nor cold, I will spit you out of my mouth. You say, 'How rich I am! And how well I have done! I have everything I want in the world.' In fact, though you do not know it, you are the most pitiful wretch, poor, blind and naked. So I advise you to buy from me gold refined in the fire, to make you truly rich, and white clothes to put on to hide the shame of your nakedness, and ointment for your eyes so that you may see. All whom I love I reprove and discipline. Be on your mettle therefore and repent. Here I stand knocking at the door; if anyone hears my voice and opens the door, I will come in and sit down to supper with him and he with me."

Revelation 3:14–20

The Need for Repentance

These words of Revelation are very typical of the attitude Jesus shows in the Gospels. Repentance was the theme of his first sermons: "Repent, and believe the gospel, for the kingdom of God is at hand." Indeed, it was the theme of the early sermons of the Apostles in Acts: "Repent," says Peter, "repent and be baptized, everyone of you, in the name of Jesus the Messiah for the forgiveness of your sins; and you will receive the gift of the Holy Spirit" (Acts 2:38).

Repentance is, indeed, the fundamental disposition of a Christian; and an abiding disposition. The first thing we must do is confess our sinfulness. No excuses, no claims, no self-complacency. And we must confess our inability to get out of our sinfulness and our absolute need for God's saving power in Jesus.

> For though the will to do good is there, the deed is not. The good which I want to do, I fail to do; but what I do is the wrong which is against my will; and if what I do is against my will, clearly it is no longer I who am the agent, but sin that has its lodging in me. I discover this principle, then: that when I want to do the right, only the wrong is within my reach. In my inmost self I delight in the law of God, but I perceive that there is in my bodily members a different law, fighting against the law that my reason approves and making me a prisoner under the law that is in my members, the law of sin. Miserable creature that I am, who is there to rescue me out of this body doomed to death? God alone, through Jesus Christ our Lord! Thanks be to God!
>
> Romans 7:18–25

It is important that the Christian experience this "miserable creature that I am, who will rescue me" of St. Paul. And which of us has not experienced this persistently in our lives? Then we can approach Jesus with no confidence in ourselves, trusting entirely in his power. He says explicitly that it is for such persons, for "sinners" that he has come, not for the "just." If we are just—self-righteous— then he hasn't come for us, he has no interest in us. We must constantly beware of this self-righteousness because it leads to the kind of blindness and hardness of heart that afflicted the Pharisees. And it is particularly difficult for us to attain this sense of our helplessness and our need of Jesus today, it seems to me, because we have largely lost the sense of sin.

The Sense of Sin

Sin is something that we play down considerably today, but it was something that Jesus seemed to give much importance to. "This is the cup of my blood, the blood of the new and everlasting covenant . . . This blood is to be shed for you and for all people that sins may be forgiven," says the priest at the most solemn moment of the Eucharist, echoing Jesus' own words. "Receive the Holy Spirit!" says Jesus to his apostles after his resurrection, "If you forgive any man's sins, they stand forgiven; if you pronounce them unforgiven, unforgiven they remain" (John 20:23). In the Lord's Prayer he bids us ask for just three things: our daily bread, moral strength to fight temptation, and forgiveness of sin. He sends his Spirit so that the Spirit may convince the world of "sin and of justice and of judgment."

There is no doubt that forgiveness of sin is something that is of vital importance to Jesus. When I talk later of the social aspect of sin, I hope to show you why. Right at the beginning of the Gospels, we are told that this is the salvation that he brings us—not primarily salvation that is economic or social or political, as it is fashionable to maintain these days, but salvation from sin.

> "Joseph, son of David," said the angel, "do not be afraid to take Mary home with you as your wife. It is by the Holy Spirit that she has conceived this child. She will bear a son; and you shall give him the name Jesus (Saviour), for he will save his people from their sins."
>
> Matthew 1:20–21

There are many other New Testament texts that underline this as the reason for God becoming human. Here are a few: "Here are words you may trust, words that merit full acceptance, 'Christ Jesus came into the world to save sinners.' " (1 Timothy 1:15). We are told in Romans 5:8 that God shows his love for us precisely in that though we were sinners, Christ died for us, and in 1 John 4–10 we are told that God sent his Son in order to be the expiation of our sins.

The forgiveness of sins is a far more vital matter to Jesus than bodily health, and material prosperity. He heals the paralytic of Matthew 9 simply as a means to show his adversaries that he has given him a far more precious grace, the forgiveness of his sins. To us, who are, perhaps, spiritually less sensitive than people of former ages, forgiveness of sin doesn't rank high on the list of desirable commodities. That is why we are in greater need of the gift of repentance.

The Meaning of Repentance

I wouldn't have you think, however, that repentance means the awareness of sin and sorrow for sin. Sorrow for sin is just one aspect of repentance—and by no means the most important one. Repentance is rendered in Greek by the word *metanoia*, which indicates a total change of heart and mind, a turning of our heart and mind away from selfishness and on to God. Perhaps the best formula for repentance is the commandment enunciated by Jesus, "Love the Lord your God with all your heart, with all your soul, with all your strength, and with all your mind; and your neighbour as yourself" (Luke 10:27). I could weep bitter tears for my sins and tell God I am deeply sorry for them and beg pardon for them. That still doesn't put me in possession of the gift of repentance. I may be far from willing to give up all my inordinate attachments and to love God totally and to lead the radically new life with the radically new attitudes that this implies. How well Jesus puts it in the passage of Revelation that I quoted earlier: Here was a person and a Church that had actually worked hard for his cause, and borne much suffering for his sake: "I know all your ways, your toil and your fortitude! . . . Fortitude you have; you have borne up in my cause and never flagged." There was also loyalty to his truth, discernment in rejecting false teachings and false apostles. Yet, the Lord is not satisfied. This Church still needs repentance, because it falls short in love. "I have this against you: You have lost your early love. Think from what a height you have fallen; repent, and do as you once did."

There is another characteristic of the grace of repentance. It is always accompanied with much joy and peace. When the theme of repentance and sorrow for sin is touched on in retreats and sermons, people generally prepare themselves for lots of "negative" feelings—feelings of guilt and self-hatred and even sadness and gloom. But anyone who confuses sadness with sorrow for sin has not experienced the sorrow for sin that comes from the Spirit. How frequently we hear people say to us after a confession of sins that they felt lightsome and happy, as though a weight had been lifted from them! Strange paradox: tears of sorrow that we have offended God coexist with sentiments of joy that we have found him again, that he loves us still, that all our sins are forgotten. And isn't that just the way it should be? When we are lost in a forest and find our way home again, when we lose a precious treasure and then recover it, isn't that cause for intense rejoicing?

Jesus always links repentance with feelings of deep joy. Very delicately he will tell us how it is the Father who rejoices when the wayward child comes home, the shepherd who rejoices when the lost sheep is found, the angels of God who rejoice at the repentance of one sinner. How much then will be the joy of the child who is once again received into the home of his Father and the sheep that finds its way into the fold and the sinners who see they have given God so much delight by returning to him! So if you have been disposing yourself to gloom and sadness when I suggested the theme of repentance for your meditation, I want you to know that it is just the opposite sentiments that you must prepare yourselves for: joy that you are going to be embraced once again by your loving Father and love, very intense love, in fact, all the love of your heart for him and for his son Jesus Christ. There is no better way I know for repenting than to repeat again and again, "My God, I do indeed love you, I want very much to love you with all my heart and mind and strength."

Repentance Follows the
Encounter with Christ

At the beginning of this conference I spoke of repentance as a means for encountering Christ. That is only partially accurate. The encounter with Christ generally precedes the grace of repentance. There is, no doubt, some initial repentance that helps us to experience Christ more deeply, but it is only after the experience that we receive the grace of repentance in all its fullness. It is only after we have met him that we understand what sin is and what love is. It is only after we have come out into the light from a dark dungeon that we understand how dark it was down there and what a precious, lovely thing light is. While we were there, our eyes had adjusted to the darkness and we might even have failed to realize that we were in darkness and in need of the light. Saint, not sinners, know what sin is, because they have come into the light of God. We know our sin through a revelation of God, not through reason.

Scripture gives us many examples of this. Paul thought he was rendering a service to God while he was persecuting the Church. It was only after his encounter with Christ that he realized his sin; then he called himself inferior to all apostles, not even worthy to be called an apostle because he persecuted the Church of Christ (1 Corinthians 15:9). He even went to the extent of calling himself the greatest of sinners (1 Timothy 1:15). But to realize all of this he had first to encounter the Lord. It was the same with Peter. He discovers who Jesus really is and then exclaims, "Depart from me, Lord, for I am a sinful man." This is also similar to the prophet Isaiah, who in his sixth chapter, describes the vision he had of God, after which he becomes keenly conscious of his sin: "Woe is me, for I am a man with polluted lips." Zacchaeus repents and is converted after the Lord comes to his house (Luke 19), and the woman (Luke 7) sheds tears of love and repentance when she meets the Lord.

And isn't this just as it should be? For how can we be sorry for offending the Lord unless we first love him? And how shall we love him unless we first come into contact with him and have some experience of him? This is why I feel that the meditation on sin and repentance is the meditation not of beginners in the spiritual life, but of the great saints, the men and women who have progressed a great deal in holiness. So it is not surprising to read that the saintly Curé D'Ars was constantly desiring to run away from his parish and become a hermit. And why? To weep for his sins, if you please! It is disconcerting and unintelligible to those of us who have not yet realized what it means to love God and be loved by him, those of us who have not yet "seen" the Lord.

There is, therefore, no need to get discouraged if you do not immediately get this extraordinary grace. The Lord is probably keeping it for you for the end, when your love for him will have deepened considerably. Content yourself now with desiring him ardently and loving him as much as you can. I once came across a prayer that is attributed to St. Anselm. I am going to give it to you here because I think it sets forth admirably the stages through which most people pass before they attain to realization of and sorrow for their sins, and all these stages are a fairly adequate description of the grace of repentance in its fullness. They are: desire for God, love of God, and hatred for sin. Here is the prayer: "O Lord our God, grant us grace to desire thee with our whole hearts; that so desiring, we may seek and find thee, and so finding thee may love thee; and loving thee, may hate those things from which thou hast redeemed us. Amen."

Some Scripture Texts

In my next conference I shall speak to you of the dangers involved in meditation on repentance and on our sinfulness. At the end of this conference I should like to offer you some of the very many texts that Scripture gives us for meditation on this subject. First, some texts from the New Testament and then some from the Old.

Luke 7: The woman of Magdala. Notice the emphasis that Jesus places on love in the forgiveness of sin. Luke 15: The parables of the loving Father, the lost coin and the lost sheep. Here the emphasis is on joy and loving kindness. Acts 9: The conversion of St. Paul. John 4: The conversion of the Samaritan woman. Luke 19: The conversion of Zacchaeus. John 21: Peter's confession of love. 1 Timothy 1:15: A very consoling passage where Paul says, in effect, if God could do such wonders in a person like me, what will he do in others who trust in him! Revelation 2:1–7 and Revelation 3:14–22: The lover shamelessly standing outside and knocking, as if he has more need of us than we of him; so similar to the shepherd going in search of the lost sheep and the loving Father waiting for his prodigal son.

The Old Testament is rich in passages for meditation on sin and repentance. I shall limit myself to some passages from the prophets: Ezekiel 16, Jeremiah 2, and Hosea 2. Isaiah 63:7–64 contains a very moving prayer that you may want to make your own.

Above all, do not try to produce the grace of repentance and sorrow for sin. Ask for it. Ask for the gift of loving God. Ask for the gift of meeting him in your prayer these days. Repentance will follow.

11

The Dangers
of Repentance

When repentance is wrongly understood, when there is an overemphasis on guilt and fear of punishment and self-hatred, then repentance becomes a very dangerous thing. All good things are dangerous and the grace of repentance is no exception. I should like, in this conference, to list some of these dangers for you.

The Refusal to Forgive Oneself

God is only too willing to forgive us. We do not even have to say we are sorry. We have only to desire to come back to him. He will not even let the prodigal son finish the little repentance speech he was making. Nothing is easier in all the world than attaining forgiveness from God. He is more eager to give forgiveness than we to receive it.

The problem is not with God but with us. For one thing, many people refuse to believe that forgiveness is something they can get so easily. And, worse still, they refuse to forgive themselves. They are constantly brooding over how miserable and wretched they have been, wishing they had never sinned, wishing they had always kept their slate clean.

They then go on to develop a false sense of unworthiness.

They are totally unworthy of God's graces. They must do penance; they must purify themselves; they must atone thoroughly for the past before they can become worthy again of God's favors. I know of no greater obstacle to progress in the spiritual life than this false sense of unworthiness. Even sin is not so great an obstacle. Sin, far from being an obstacle, is a positive help, if there is repentance. But this false sense of unworthiness (this refusal, on our part, to forget the past and push on into the future) makes it just impossible for us to make any progress at all. I knew a priest who had lapsed grievously after his ordination. I was convinced that, in prayer, God was giving him extraordinary graces, that God was inviting him to high contemplation. But it was impossible to convince this priest of that. He was a despicable sinner in his own eyes; he was unworthy; anything that seemed like a special grace from God was suspect and an illusion—just pride appearing in a subtle form. The grace of God can triumph over sin easily; over this form of resistance it can triumph only with the greatest difficulty!

Let me give you another example, this one of a seminarian who was plagued with a sexual difficulty that he was trying, with all good will but little success, to overcome. While talking with him one day, I suddenly discovered that his whole notion of God was entirely pagan. Here he was, a seminarian, with some training in theology, and he hadn't as yet heard the good news. The God he was dealing with was the God of reason, or the God of any other religion you please, not the Father of Our Lord Jesus Christ. He was obsessed with a sense of his unworthiness, with the need to purify himself and do penance before he could approach this all-holy God of his and establish loving relations with him. I had a fantasy of him while he was talking and I shared it with him. I said to him, I see you as a woman who has been disloyal to her husband and turned prostitute. She is now sorry for her sins and has returned home. But she dare not enter the house. She stands outside, in the street, in sackcloth and ashes, determined to do penance for her sins. And there she stands, day after day, for weeks and months on end. Of what good is that penance of hers to her husband? He wants her love again, he wants to feel the warmth of her body and enjoy her caresses. But the woman is obstinate in first "purifying" herself—or, perhaps, she is just too afraid to take the risk of walking right into the house, to embrace her husband and tell him she loves him still. The seminarian listened to me attentively, then he said slowly, "That's just what I am. I don't dare go in. I'm too scared to take the risk. I might be rejected." I said to him, "Would you be able to go to the chapel now and, forgetting all your sins and sexual difficulties, just look at the Lord and say, Lord I love you with all my heart?" "No, I wouldn't dare do that." "Well, try doing it right here. We shall both pray silently for a while. And let us both forget our sins and center our hearts on the Lord and tell him that we love him." That is what we did for about five minutes. It was a very moving experience for him and for me.

Many of us have yet to learn that repentance doesn't mean saying, "Lord, I'm sorry" (I was impressed by the sentence in that delightful novel *Love Story*, "Love means never having to say you're sorry"), but, "Lord, I love you with all my heart." Have you noticed that nowhere in the New Testament does Jesus tell us that in order to get forgiveness for our sins we must be sorry? He is not, obviously, excluding sorrow for sin. He just doesn't explicitly demand it. Whereas we have made such a fuss about contrition, and how many penitents I have had who were bothered to distraction about whether they had sufficient contrition, whether their contrition was "perfect" or "imperfect" and such other largely irrelevant questions as far as forgiveness is concerned. And while we got lost in what Jesus did not explicitly demand of us, we conveniently overlooked the things that he explicitly and insistently demanded. He said, "If you want forgiveness from my heavenly Father, then you must forgive your brother." That one condition was conspicuously absent from the conditions for a "good confession" that were listed in our old catechism books. We were quite meticulous about examining our consciences and telling all our sins to the priest and making an act of contrition and a purpose of amendment and fulfilling the penance enjoined us. We were not explicitly told that more important by far than all of these, was that we forgive our brothers and sisters any wrong they have done us. Indeed, we were not told that if this were missing, our sins were simply not forgiven, no matter how perfect our contrition or how accurate our recital of our sins to the priest in the confessional. There's another thing that Jesus demanded of us if we would have our sins forgiven: love. As simple as that. Come to me and say you love me and your sins will be forgiven. We are accustomed to think of those tears of the woman of Magdala as tears of sorrow for sin. I wonder where we got that notion in the face of Jesus' explicit statement that her tears and all she was doing were expressions of her love. Many sins are forgiven her *because* she has loved much. After Peter's denial of Jesus, this is what Jesus demands of him: an expression of love. "Simon, son of John, do you love me more than all else?" This is precisely what repentance is all about, and if we would be keenly aware of this we would be spared all the discouragement and sadness and even excessive fear of God that many people feel when they dwell on their sinfulness and seek the grace of repentance. I advise you to spend some time with Our Lord after this conference, a time of repentance in which you just tell him again and again as Peter did, "Lord, you know all things, you know I love you."

This brings me to another characteristic of the Christian God I was speaking of earlier, as opposed to the God of reason and all other gods; a characteristic of the good news that Jesus preached, as opposed to the tenets of rational, sober religion. The characteristic is this: for Jesus, even though to sin is the greatest conceivable evil, to be a sinner is a value. Hate sin with all your heart and avoid it. But if you have sinned and (this is important) repent, then you have reason to rejoice, because there is greater joy in heaven over the sinner who repents than over ninety-nine who have no need of repentance. Who can understand this kind of madness? The kind of madness that seizes the Church when, on the vigil of Easter, she speaks of the sin of Adam as a "necessary sin," as a "happy fault," because it brought us our savior Jesus Christ. The Church is only echoing what St. Paul says to the Romans. Where sin abounded, grace superbounded. He obviously sees the value of our having sinned. Then he draws the logical conclusion from this idea. Why not sin deliberately so that we shall receive even more grace? And he recoils from this conclusion in horror. God forbid, he says. We are dealing here with a mystery that is beyond the comprehension of the human mind. It is important to maintain the truth of both these opposites. Hate sin. And, if you have sinned and repented, consider yourself very lucky indeed because grace is going to be poured into you in superabundant measure. The repentant sinner (the sinner who returns to God in love) draws God to himself with greater force than a magnet. God finds him not loathsome, but irresistible. That is the good news. The other stuff about being sorry and making atonement for our sins isn't good news at all. It is stale news. We knew it all along without the benefit of Jesus' proclamation.

The Excessive Fear of God

Excessive fear of God is another bad effect of meditation on our sinfulness when it isn't properly made: an excessive fear of God and of his punishment. I am impressed by the vast number of Christians, even and especially priests, who are full of fear of God. They are still trapped within a religion of law, twenty centuries after Jesus preached a God who was love itself and a liberation from the burden of the law. These are not necessarily scrupulous people, and often they are not even conscious of this fear that rules their spiritual lives. But their dealings with God are characterised by one big round of duties. If there is ever any danger of death, the first thing they will want to do is rush to confession—the sacrament of reconciliation is used by them for purposes that are totally alien to the mentality of Jesus: to get a guarantee that will allow them to stand before God blameless, to "protect" themselves from God and his judgment. It has never occurred to them how repugnant is the very notion that Christians, no matter how sinful, should seek to protect themselves from their heavenly Father. The underlying fear that prompted so many priests to say their breviary in the old days is a good example of this. (As is also the fear that brought and still brings many Catholics to mass on Sunday—and then we violently reject any accusation that our religion is a religion of law, fully a match for the religion of the Pharisees that Jesus attacked in his teachings.) It was believed in the old days that to omit even one of the small hours of the breviary was a mortal sin (meaning, your heavenly Father would throw you into hell for that offense—and don't come to argue with me after this conference, because I know all the arguments about the fruit being a small thing, but the disobedience of Adam and Eve being the really criminal thing. I am perfectly aware how, in our neurotic desire to control people by increasing the number of mortal sins, we allowed our reason to draw the most absurd "logical" conclusions). One victim of this old mentality was a priest who prayed faithfully for twenty years of his priestly life, never omitting his breviary or his meditation or his examination of conscience. But there was such a joylessness in his prayer and his dealings with God in general. He once said to me sadly, "I sometimes get the irrational feeling that if there were no commandments, I would be a saint. I'd feel so free and liberated—and I know I would keep everyone of those commandments spontaneously." I was reminded of a Jesuit friend of mine who told me that he never realized how much he enjoyed study until he entered the religious life. At home he had a mother who nagged him so much into study that he was "forced" to do under constraint and with distaste what he would have done with real relish and enjoyment had he been left free. I am also reminded of another Jesuit, a seminarian, who was a very fervent person, a kind of model religious, but who seemed perpetually sad, in spite of his, to me, artificial attempts at jollity. One day, in a moment of deep insight, the root of his sadness was unearthed. He found himself saying to this

God whom he was serving with all his heart and soul, "God, I really hate you. You are a kill-joy. I just cannot enjoy life while you are around. You won't allow me. You won't leave me free." There is (or at least has been) something very, very, very wrong with our understanding of Jesus and his message.

To deal with this neurotic fear of God we need another understanding of law and its place in our life. I am not advocating the abolition of law, but another understanding of it. The problem is not the demands that the law makes. (People who want to rid themselves of the demands of the law and live under the Spirit in the hope that they will then be able to live comfortably ever after, have no notion at all of the pains that freedom brings and of the loving demands that the Spirit makes—far greater than anything that law would ever dream of!) So the problem is not the demands that the law makes. It is law in as much as it breeds fear and in as much as it binds and renders us incapable to serving God freely. So a fresh understanding of the law is necessary if we are to respond in love and freedom to the God whom Jesus proclaimed.

There's something else that is necessary: a better understanding of God's love for us, a love that is unconditional. Have you observed the type of love a good mother has for her children? She doesn't love them because they are good. She loves them because they are her children. She obviously wants them to be good, she wants them to improve. A mother whose son is a criminal will want him to give up his evil ways. But, being a mother, she doesn't cease to love him. She will not say, "First stop being a criminal and then I will love you." She says, "I hate your criminal ways, but I still love you very intensely because you are my son." If there is any hope of the boy changing, it is because of this unconditional love of his mother for him. Do we dare to think that this is the way God loves us?

Scripture scholars tell us of the difference between the messages of the Old Testament and the New. Put crudely, in the Old Testament God said, if you are good and obedient, I shall be kind to you; if you are rebellious, I shall be angry with you and destroy you. Jesus shows us a different God, so to speak, one who is good to saints and sinners alike, who gives to both the benefits of his rain and his sunshine and his love. God's love is not limited to those people who fulfil certain conditions, any more than a mother's love is limited to those children who keep all the rules she imposes. To preach this kind of God, as Jesus did, is a very dangerous business. People will tend to take advantage of his goodness. But that is the way with all love: it takes the risk, it leaves itself vulnerable to being taken advantage of—how else will it win the love of the other? And this is the risk that Jesus was ready to take and did indeed take when he showed us the true nature of his Father.

When I was a novice, our novice master would say to us, "The red letter day in your spiritual life will come, not when you believe that you love God, but when you realize that he loves you!" Many years of experience (experience of others and my own) have shown me how right he was. What a transformation occurs in our lives, how rapidly we begin to change, when we realize how much and how unconditionally he loves and accepts us! I read of a Protestant pastor who seemed to have the charism of mediating an encounter with Christ precisely through mediating to the other person the experience of Christ's unconditional love. Someone would say to him, "I'd like to meet Christ. How and where can I meet him?" This pastor would take this person to some quiet place where they were not likely to be disturbed and say something like this to him or her (I am giving you the details as nearly as I can remember them because I am going to recommend that you do the same thing for yourselves later), "I want you to close your eyes and listen carefully to what I say: Jesus Christ, the Risen Lord, is present here with us. Do you believe this?" After a period of silence the person would reply, "Yes, I believe this." "Now listen to something that may be harder for you to believe," the pastor would continue. "Listen carefully: Jesus Christ, the Risen Lord, loves and accepts you just as you are. You don't have to change. You don't have to become better.

You don't even have to get out of your sin. You don't have to do this in order to get his love. You have it already, right now, in whatever condition you are. In fact, we know how intense his love is for us precisely because he loves us when we are sinners and is even ready to die for us. Do you believe this?" A much longer pause occurs generally before the person says, "Yes. I believe that Jesus who is here loves me just as I am." "Then," says the pastor, "say something to Jesus. Say it aloud." The person doesn't pray for long before grasping the pastor's hand and saying, "You are right. He *is* here! I can sense his presence!"

I am not recommending this as an infallible way for mediating the experience of Christ's presence to everyone. This may have been a special charism possessed by this pastor. However, I have recommended this exercise to people with very, very good results. I remember offering this exercise to a large group of nearly two hundred seminarians and priests in retreat during a Holy Hour service on the eve of the Feast of the Sacred Heart. I told them to take a few minutes to remind themselves of the presence of the Risen Lord there in the chapel, then to spend some time in letting the other truth sink in—that Jesus loves and accepts all of us just as we are—and then to pour their hearts out to the Lord in loving prayer. Many of them told me that it was certainly the most effective prayer they made in that whole retreat. One community of sisters practiced this exercise as a group and told me that it brought them extraordinary spiritual graces.

In spite of a deep-rooted reluctance I have for giving credence to visions and revelations, not excluding the revelations pertaining to the devotion to the Heart of Christ made to Margaret Mary, I am a great believer in the efficacy of this devotion and am willing to accept these revelations as an instance of the gift of prophecy that Christ continues to exercise in order to communicate with his Church down the centuries. He is reported to have said that those who practice this devotion will experience untold benefits in their spiritual lives—sinners will be given the grace of conversion, saints will make extraordinary progress in holiness. Priests and others who propagate this devotion are told that they will experience in their apostolate fruits beyond their wildest expectations. All of this makes perfect sense to me. Please do not confuse devotion to the Heart of Christ with the many devotions that have been inflicted upon us—tiresome and sentimental as so many of them were. Do not even confuse it with the symbol of the pierced heart, which appeals to some and disgusts others. The essence of this devotion, as I see it, is to accept that love which the Father has for us in Christ, to accept the fact that Jesus loves us unconditionally, that he is love itself. If you accept this truth in your own life and help others to accept it, you cannot but experience extraordinary results in your own spiritual life and in your apostolate.

We often ask ourselves, "What have I done for Christ? What shall I do for Christ?" Rarely do we realize that the finest thing we could do for him is believe in his love for us. Have you ever had the experience of someone you love very much saying to you, "I cannot quite believe that you really love me?" If you have, then you will know that what we want most from those we love, more than all the service they can offer us, is that they believe in our love, that they love us in return and that they value this love that we are offering them. This, to me, is what the devotion to the Sacred Heart is all about. How badly the world is in need of it today!

Experiencing Christ as a Demand

This is the final danger involved in the meditation on repentance and on our sinfulness. Christ is frequently experienced by people as a demand long before he is experienced as a gift. And the call to repentance frequently heightens this sense that Christ is a demand, the demanding God, always asking for more and more and more, insatiable, never satisfied, no matter how much one gives or does.

This is best illustrated, I think, by the prayer someone once

made. It ran something like this, "Lord, I want to receive your
Holy Spirit. But I am afraid to ask you for him, because I am afraid
of the demands he will make on me. Help me, Lord to overcome
my fears." I was more than a little scandalized by this prayer. And
the tragedy is that this prayer is one that many others share in: the
fear of coming too close to God, the fear of his demands on us. The
Holy Spirit is the Father's gift to us—and we are afraid of this gift!
We are afraid of the strings that will be attached to this gift when it
comes!

Imagine a loving Father bringing toys home for his children.
He walks in eagerly, unwraps the toys and offers them to the kids—
who stand back, fearful to accept the toys. They know their father;
this is a bribe; he's going to make demands on them afterwards;
they will have to pay the price for the joy these toys bring. They'd
rather not have the toys. Isn't this the way we treat our heavenly
Father? We can hardly bring ourselves to believe that the offers he
makes to us come without any strings attached, that all he wants is
our happiness and peace.

Perhaps we are not entirely to blame for this. We have been
brought up to believe that God is a demanding God rather than a
loving Father who loves us unconditionally. The best way to correct that notion is to stop measuring up to the demands, real or
imaginary, that we think God is making on us. Do not give in to
the demands of the beloved, give in only to the demands of the love
in your own heart. If you ignore the love in your own heart and
strive to give more than you have the love for, you will end up by
either feeling guilty or resentful. Far from increasing your love, this
will make it diminish.

This will become clear if I give you an example. Let us imagine a boy, John, who is passionately in love with Mary. In an excess
of love he will sometimes forego lunch and, with his lunch money,
buy flowers to present to Mary in the evening. Love does crazy
things like this. Love even grows on gestures like these. Now imagine that Henry comes to me for help because he is finding it hard

to feel love for his wife, Jane. And I say to him, "Why don't you imitate John? Forgo your lunch and with the money you save buy flowers for Jane." Instead of recapturing this love for Jane, he is only likely to build up a resentment against her. Slavishly imitating the behavior of a lover without possessing those inner dispositions is no formula for becoming a lover oneself. You can see the danger involved in our telling our novices to imitate the behavior of the saints when they do not as yet have in their hearts the love of God that inspired that behavior. We sometimes urge them on in the fond hope that the behavior will automatically produce the love. But there is no evidence for this at all; quite the contrary. They are likely to end up discouraged and to give the whole thing up.

God never demands of you more than what the love you feel for him in you heart demands. If you want to do the great deeds that the saints did for him, then ask him to pour into your heart the love that the saints had for him. As your love for him grows, so will your ability to give yourself to him cheerfully. God loves a cheerful giver. Constraint and force do not last very long. A priest once said to me, "One morning at meditation, I realized as never before that God loves me unconditionally. I think I made more progress in that one day than I did in twenty years of living up to God's demands, or what I thought were God's demands on me." Very true. Ask Jesus to give you the experience of his love for you. Your generosity in doing great things for him will then take care of itself; it will follow automatically.

12

The Social
Aspect of Sin

In this brief conference I want to speak to you of an aspect of sin that appeals to the modern mind. In former days saints were deeply moved to contrition at the contemplation of Christ on the Cross and the thought that it is sin, their sin, that had crucified him. Today I think people are more moved at the crucifixion of Christ that goes on today as a result of sin.

Am I Responsible for My
Brother's and Sister's Suffering?

It is our belief that all suffering has come into this world as a result of sin. And the more sin there is, the more suffering. Jesus is on his cross today again in the person of his brothers and sisters: the victims of injustice, the sick, the emotionally ill. Just as I could stand in front of the crucified Christ and say, "My sin has done this," so I can stand before anyone who is suffering today and say, "My sin has done this." That is the reason why we confessed our sin not only to God but also to our brothers and sisters. It is not God alone that we hurt by our sin, but the whole mystical body. Father Teilhard puts it well. He says, "Strike the bronze gong in one place and the whole gong reverberates." For better or for worse, we are all part of one body; if one member of the body is diseased the rest of the body suffers too.

Someone once told the Hindu saint, Swami Ramdas, that an agnostic man in the West had said, "I do not believe in God. If I did, I would seek him out and strangle him for all the suffering he has caused in the world." Ramdas replied, "If I were to meet this man, I would gently place his hands at his throat and say, go ahead; here is the one who is causing the suffering; strangle him." It is customary for us today to blame the evils in the world and the Church on others. It isn't really the liberals or the conservatives who are to blame for the turmoil and confusion in the Church. It isn't the capitalists and the communists who are responsible for the suffering and the injustice in the world. It is sin. My sin. If we would eradicate sin, we would eradicate suffering.

If we accept this truth, we will see how important it is to work for the eradication of sin in the world. We have plunged wholeheartedly into the work of eradicating hunger and unemployment and disease and illiteracy. Excellent! This is a work of compassion. This is what our Christian love demands of us. If we are coldhearted towards our suffering and under-privileged brothers and sisters, our preaching is meaningless, we do not have Christ's love in our hearts.

But we may never forget that in doing this work it is the symptoms that we are tackling; we have also to work on the root. An anaesthetic will kill the pain that a cancer patient feels; it will not kill the cancer. No more will the eradication of hunger and disease and illiteracy kill the cancer of selfishness at the root of all these evils. Witness the nations of the West where some of these symptoms have been successfully eradicated. Are they happier, more selfless, more loving? In fact, is there less suffering there than in the underdeveloped countries? We have achieved little if we have not come to grips with the problem of selfishness and sin.

It is easier to understand now why Jesus seemed to pay such little attention to the social and political problems of his time and to give so much importance to sin and the forgiveness of sin. A very social-minded seminarian who worked among the refugees of Bangladesh came back from those scenes of misery and starvation and said to me, "I have realized that the greatest evil in the world is not that a man should die of hunger. That is a painful death, no doubt; but people die equally painful deaths, I imagine, in affluent societies when they die of cancer, and modern medicine is unable to kill the pain. No, the really horrible thing is not the pain of starvation; the horrible thing is the callousness and indifference of the man who could help his starving brother and will not." The horror of selfishness and of sin!

The social apostolate is thought of today as being work to uplift the poor, the eradication of social injustice. We rarely think of the work a priest does in the confessional and in the proclamation of the Word as being social apostolate. We are losing sight of the importance of reconciling sinners to God. May not this be part of the identity crisis that so many priests are undergoing today, the crisis I spoke of to you at the beginning of this conference? It is frequently a crisis of superficiality. It springs from the belief that the primary task of the priest in the modern world is involvement—involvement in revolution, politics, and social uplift. By these standards Jesus was very "uninvolved." He never gives the impression that he is primarily concerned with the social and political issues of his times; quite to the contrary, he stubbornly refuses to allow himself to be drawn into them.

The modern priest, like Jesus, must concern himself primarily with preaching the good news. Let him work by all means, in education and social uplift. But let him not fail to proclaim repentance to humankind, calling on them to admit that they are sinners, and to accept God's gracious love. I am reminded here of a saying of John Wesley, the founder of the Methodists: "Give me a hundred men," he said, "who desire nothing but God and fear nothing but sin, and I shall shake the gates of hell and establish the kingdom of God on earth." That sentence could lend itself to a very fruitful exercise of prayer. Make a list, in God's presence, of all the things you desire. Does God come first on the list? Of all things you fear and hate, does sin come first? If they do, you certainly have the grace of repentance in great abundance!

Confession

I would like to say a few words at the end of this conference on what we have traditionally called the sacrament of confession. I prefer the word used by modern authors, the sacrament of reconciliation, or the sacrament of repentance. Many retreatants in the past have told me that receiving this sacrament has been a great help, even a turning point, in their retreat. It might do for you what it has done for them.

Priests have sometimes told me that they hardly ever receive this sacrament because it brings no improvement in their lives. "What's the use of confessing the same old sins and defects time after time? There seems to be no improvement, and I feel like a hypocrite. If I were sincere in my repentance, those sins should disappear, shouldn't they?"

The assumption here is that the primary aim of this sacrament is the removal of sins and defects, an assumption I do not agree with. The primary aim of this sacrament is reconciliation with God, a deeper union with Christ, a fresh infusion of the power of the Holy Spirit. And so, the dispositions with which we approach this sacrament are more important than that list of sins we confess, and these graces I have just mentioned are more important than the removal of defects. Christ may will us to have these defects all our lives so that his power may shine out in our weakness. They will not prevent us from growing in holiness or from getting the spiritual treasures this sacrament offers.

If we are to draw profit from this sacrament, we must approach it with proper dispositions. So far there has been a concern, an over-concern, to examine our consciences and make as accurate a list of our sins as possible. This is of secondary importance compared with the dispositions I am going to enumerate now.

The first thing we must do is forgive others all the wrong others have done us. Jesus brings this out forcefully in the parable of the unforgiving servant (Matthew 18), and also in the Sermon on the Mount when he says,

> If, when you are bringing your gift to the altar, you suddenly remember that your brother has a grievance against you, leave your gift where it is before the altar. First go and make your peace with your brother, and only then come back and offer your gift. . . . This is how you should pray: Our Father in heaven . . . forgive us the wrong we have done, as we have forgiven those who have wronged us. . . . For if you forgive others the wrongs they have done, your heavenly Father will also forgive you; but if you do not forgive others, then the wrongs you have done will not be forgiven by your Father.
>
> Matthew 5:23–24; 6:14–15

Finally, in Mark 11:25 he says,

> And when you stand praying, if you have a grievance against anyone, forgive him, so that your Father in heaven may forgive you the wrongs you have done.

In a previous conference I have dealt with this topic of forgiving our brothers and sisters the wrongs they have done us and suggested some exercises in prayer for this purpose. You may want to use one or other of these exercises as a preparation for the sacrament of reconciliation.

Another disposition we must bring to this sacrament is the acknowledgment of our sinfulness. This was Jesus' complaint against the Pharisees. They would not see their sinfulness and their need of him. The parable of the pharisee and the publican (Luke 18) is a clear example of this. So are Jesus' words to the Pharisees in Matthew 9:12–13: "It is not the healthy that need a doctor, but the sick. . . . I did not come to invite virtuous people, but sinners." See how Paul insists on this same disposition in Romans, Chapters 2 and 3. St. John does the same:

> If we claim to be sinless, we are self-deceived and strangers to the truth. If we confess our sins, he is just, and may be trusted to forgive our sins and cleanse us from every kind of wrong; but if we say we have committed no sin, we make him out to be a liar, and then his word has no place in us.
>
> 1 John 1:8–10

And in the Book of Revelation, John puts these words into the mouth of Jesus,

> You say, "How rich I am! And how well I have done! I have everything I want in the world." In fact, though you do not know it, you are the most pitiful wretch, poor, blind, and naked. So I advise you to buy from me gold refined in the fire, to make you truly rich, and white clothes to put on to hide the shame of your nakedness, and ointment for your eyes so that you may see. . . . Be on your mettle and repent.
>
> Revelation 3:17–19

Yet another disposition we must bring to this sacrament is a great love for Jesus and a great desire to see him. I have dealt with this theme when I spoke earlier about the meaning of repentance. Remember the demand that Jesus makes of the Church of Ephesus that it come back to its early love (Revelation 2:1–5); the eager longing of Zacchaeus (Luke 19); the loving tears of the woman of Magdala (Luke 7) and Peter's confession of love for Jesus (John 21).

One final disposition to bring to this sacrament is a belief in Jesus' great desire to forgive us. He brings this out forcefully in his parables of the loving father, the lost coin, the lost sheep (Luke 15) and in his words in the book of Revelation: "Here I stand knocking at the door; if anyone hears my voice and opens the door, I will come in and sit down to supper with him and he with me" (Revelation 3:20). Anyone! No matter how sinful you are. All you need do is hear his voice and open the door to him!

Having spoken of these dispositions, let me suggest a way of receiving this sacrament during this retreat that others have found helpful and that you may want to try. For one thing, you may wish to sit down rather than kneel if you think this will help you to be more at ease and to speak at greater leisure.

You may begin by thanking God for some of the graces he has given you. Doing this before the priest is a witness before the Church's representative of your gratitude to God who has been so good to you. Gratitude will also dispose you to a greater realization of God's love for you and to a deeper experience of repentance.

After you have mentioned your sins, I suggest you ask for healing in some areas of your life. Mention any illness, physical, emotional, or spiritual that you wish the Lord to cure you of. The forgiveness of sins was linked by the Lord with healing and the sacrament of reconciliation is also a sacrament of healing. The reason why we do not experience this more frequently is that we do not expect it to occur. Together with healing you will frequently notice a fresh upsurge of spiritual power in you as a result of receiving this sacrament. For, with the forgiveness of sins, we are also given a fresh infusion of the Holy Spirit.

Then, if the priest agrees, you and he could spend a brief while in prayer, silent or vocal, asking that through the power of the absolution you are going to receive, the Lord may heal you and give you renewed strength in his service.

I trust that when you receive the sacrament of reconciliation during this retreat, the Lord will reveal to you the power that he has placed in it and that he gives so generously to those who accept this sacrament with faith and devotion.

13

The Benedictine Method of Prayer

In the previous conferences I have often given you passages from Scripture for meditation and reflection. I should now like to offer you a method of using Scripture in your prayer, a way of converting the scripture passages into prayer. This is a method of prayer that has come to be known as the Benedictine Method because it was popularized by St. Benedict; it has been in use in the Church for centuries. You will probably find it extremely useful, particularly if you tend to be distracted easily in prayer and don't know what to do with yourself when distractions come.

There are three stages in this method of prayer: Lectio, Meditatio, and Oratio. Lectio is the *lectio divina*, the reading. You begin by reading a passage from Scripture or from some spiritual book. I advise you not to take to prayer any book that you haven't previously read. There is the danger that you will be carried away by curiosity (which can sometimes be a subtle form of laziness) and spend most of your time in reading rather than in praying. Let's suppose you have begun by reading a passage from Scripture or from a book like *The Imitation of Christ*. You keep on reading until you come to a sentence or phrase that appeals to you. You are reading, let us say John 7:

> On the last and greatest day of the festival Jesus stood and cried
> aloud, "If anyone is thirsty let him come to me; whoever be-
> lieves in me, let him drink. As Scripture says, 'Streams of liv-
> ing water shall flow out from within him.'"

Those words of Jesus appeal to you. Then this is the place to stop
your reading, to end the Lectio and move on to Meditatio, the
meditation.

Meditation is done with one's mouth, not with one's mind.
This is not a matter of reflection and discursive thought but a repetition of these words either vocally or mentally. When the psalmist
says in Psalm 118 that he will constantly meditate on the law of
God and that he finds this law sweet to his tongue, sweeter than
honey and the honeycomb, he isn't just talking of reflection on the
law, but also of ceaseless repetition of the words of the law. So this
is what you must do with those words you have chosen. Recite
them interiorly and relish them while you recite them without
stopping to make any deep reflection upon them. You will do
something like this: "If any are thirsty, let them come to me . . . If
any are thirsty, let them come to me . . . If any are thirsty let them
come to me . . ." As you go along you will tend to emphasize some
words over others and your sentence will grow shorter: "Any . . .
Any . . . Any . . ." or, "Come to me . . . Come to me . . . Come to
me . . ." Keep on repeating these words as long as the repetition
brings you savor and relish. Then stop and enter the third phase,
the oratio, the phase of prayer.

As you keep on repeating those words a time will come when
you will want to stop and dwell on them silently or say something
to the Lord. This is what the *oratio* is. You may say something like,
"Lord, are you making this offer to anyone? Just anyone, with no
distinction between saints and sinners? Then I am coming to you
with great confidence." Or, "How right you are, Lord, that the
place to come to when our heart is thirsty is you. I wish I had done

it more frequently in my life. I should have been a happier person. But I'm coming now." Or, "This just doesn't make sense to me Lord. How are you going to slake our thirst? How often I have come to you in the past, and I'm still thirsty. What do these words of yours mean? Tell me." Or, as I said before, you will not want to speak to the Lord but just be silent in his presence, letting those words sink into you, letting yourself rest lovingly in the presence of the Lord who has said those words.

This is an ideal way of reciting the Psalms. There are hundreds of sentences in the Psalms where we will want to rest and nourish ourselves. I advise you to do this when you recite your breviary. So many priests are more concerned with getting through their morning or evening prayer than with really praying. Why not do this? If you normally take fifteen minutes for your morning prayer, then don't force yourself to finish the prayer within that time. Dwell lovingly on any phrase that leads you to prayer in the Psalms or hymns or scripture reading that you find in the breviary. And, having done this for fifteen minutes, end your morning prayer. You will not have "finished" your morning prayer, but you will have prayed. You will not have kept the letter of the law but you will have observed the spirit. That is what the Church wants the priest to do: to really pray, not just cover a certain number of pages each day.

While I am on this subject, I want to say something about another form of prayer that is attributed to St. John Commacus, the great Greek master. He is reputed to have initiated dozens of monks into the art of prayer by this simple method of his. He would get them to take a prayer formula, the Lord's Prayer, for instance, and to recite it with perfect attention, slowly, mindful of what they were saying and to whom they were saying the words. Let's suppose you begin to say the Our Father and are attending to each word you are saying and to the fact that it is the Father you are addressing. "Our." And let's suppose that at this point your mind begins to wander. Then, when you realize you are wandering, bring your mind back to the words at which it began to wander. "Your kingdom come . . . Your kingdom come . . ." And keep at it until you say these words too with attention. Then move on, "Your will be done on earth as it is in heaven," etc. It doesn't matter whether you feel devotion or not while you are reciting this prayer. The important thing is that you say it attentively. The devotion will come of itself.

St. Ignatius of Loyola recommends yet another method, which combines meditation with vocal prayer. Here you dwell on each word you are saying, but take time out to reflect on the meaning of each word. What does Father mean? Why do we call God, "Father"? Why do we use the word "our" when we say "Our Father"? In the Hail Holy Queen, I could ask myself, why do we call Mary "Queen"? Whose Queen is she? In what sense is she a queen? We call her Holy Queen. In what sense is she Holy? What is the meaning of holiness? And so with the other words, *Our life, our sweetness, our hope*, etc. Once you have done this with a prayer, you will find that the whole prayer comes alive when you recite it. You may try this method with prayers that you frequently say: the Our Father, the Hail Mary, the Glory be, grace before and after meals, the prayers of the Mass.

These are simple ways of praying—too simple for some of us, but very effective if we are to make progress in the art of prayer. I have told you already how I learned from Father Calveras that vocal prayer properly made can be the antechamber to mysticism. This was very much the teaching of St. Teresa and the other saints who used very simple forms of prayer. In fact, it is a sign of progress in prayer when our prayer moves from the realm of the mind and comes to the heart, when it becomes more simple and more affective. St. Teresa was a great advocate for praying with the heart rather than the mind. She says she could never do much thinking in her prayer; she would be immediately distracted; so much so that for years she never dared to go to prayer without having a book with her, so that she could lean upon it whenever she need to, to deal with her distractions. But she looks upon this proneness of her mind to wander as a real blessing because she was forced to pray with her heart. She would spend her time loving God rather than thinking of him. It is to this that she attributes the great progress she made in prayer.

This is what she says in her Interior Castle of the Soul: "I only want you to be warned that if you would make much progress in the area and ascend to the mansions of your choice, the important thing is not to think much but to love much." And in her Way of Perfection she says: "There are some who think that the whole thing lies in thought and if they cannot think they feel they are wasting their time."

Unfortunately, in our prayer lives, we cultivate our minds far more diligently than our hearts. This is one of the chief reasons why we draw such little benefit from prayer. The mind is obviously needed for prayer. We need it to grasp God's word, to listen to what God has to say to us. But merely being occupied with some truth or reflection will not nourish and strengthen us. If we are to come into contact with God we need the heart. In fact we need the heart even for understanding the wisdom regarding the truths of God that the mind alone cannot give us. Let us think, by all means, but let us not give most of our prayer time to thought; it shouldn't be long before we quieten our minds, cease from our thinking and awaken our hearts to love God, to rest in his loving presence, to trust in him, worship him, unite ourselves with him. And for this I trust you will find some of these simple methods of prayer I have suggested in this conference very useful.

14

The Kingdom of Christ

In the last conference I offered you the theme of repentance for your prayer and meditation. I should like to offer you another theme today, once again developing an idea from Jesus' first sermons: "Repent and believe the gospel, for the kingdom of God is at hand."

After repenting and turning from ourselves to God, after a change of heart and mind, we ask as St. Paul did, "Lord what do you want me to do for you?" And the answer we receive from him is: "Believe the gospel. Come follow me. Be my disciple. For the kingdom of God is at hand." So there is a kingdom. And there is a king! This is the theme I should like to offer you now.

Right at the beginning of the Gospels we find this theme of the kingship of Christ. The angel says to Mary, "He will be great; he will bear the title 'Son of the Most High'; the Lord God will give him the throne of his ancestor David, and he will be king over Israel for ever; his reign shall never end." We are told here clearly that Jesus is king and that he will reign as king.

So we search the Gospels to find this kingship of Christ, and for a long time we search in vain. We discover the preacher, the wonder-worker, the friend of sinners. But of the king there is no trace at all. In fact, he is constantly avoiding the title when people want to give it to him, and he seems to be frequently covering up the fact that he is the Messiah, whom the Jews looked upon as a kind of religious king. We finally stumble upon him in the pretorium and hear him saying these words to Pilate: "Yes, I am a king. My kingdom is not of this world" (John 18). Here he says it openly, "I am a king." When he is a prisoner and helpless, he chooses to openly proclaim his kingship. We find him hailed as king again on the cross—Jesus of Nazareth, King of the Jews—and when he is bullied and ridiculed by the soldiers who kneel before him mockingly and say, "Hail, King" and slap him or spit upon him. "My kingdom is not of this world!" What a perfect image of Christ's kingship that is: him sitting there, a prisoner being made fun of, a mock crown on his head, a mock scepter in his hands, a mock robe of purple on his shoulders, and mock subjects kneeling before him in scorn and ridicule!

I suggest that you dwell on this scene in your prayer today. It will tell you a great deal about the nature of this king and his kingdom. And while you dwell on this scene, listen to those haunting words of his: "The Messiah was bound to suffer thus before entering his glory" (Luke 24:25). Or take Matthew 16:20ff., which eloquently tells the secret of Christ's kingship. Peter has just made his confession that Jesus is the Messiah. Once Jesus sees that his heavenly Father has revealed to Peter that he is the Messiah, he begins to instruct them on the meaning of his messiahship, his kingship, lest they think of this title in a worldly way.

> From that time Jesus began to make it clear to his disciples that he had to go to Jerusalem, and there to suffer much from the elders, chief priests, and lawyers; to be put to death and to be raised again on the third day. At this Peter took him by the arm and began to rebuke him: "Heaven forbid!" he said. "No, Lord, this shall never happen to you." Then Jesus turned and said to Peter, "Away with you, Satan; you are a stumbling block to me. You think as men think, not as God thinks!"

Peter simply couldn't make any sense of this kind of kingship. And the violence of Jesus' reaction seems to point to the fact that he himself was tempted by Satan. It was probably hard for him too, to make sense out of this kind of kingship, to think as God thinks, not as human beings think. He too was human, after all, and must have rebelled against the thought that this salvation he was going to offer the world would be offered in an obscure, underdeveloped country where he wouldn't even be recognized by his own and where he would die on the cross unable to come down and make good the claim that he was the son of God—in other words, that he would be a glorious failure and a laughing stock to the people who really mattered. Wasn't this what the devil was taunting him about and tempting him with when he was in the desert? To save the world in a somewhat more sensible way, a way that made better sense to those who think as human beings think rather than as God thinks? But Jesus successfully overcame those temptations. What he said does not apply only to himself, but to everyone who intends to follow him.

> Jesus then said to his disciples, "If anyone wishes to be a follower of mine, he must leave self behind; he must take up his cross and come with me. Whoever cares for his own safety is lost; but if a man will let himself be lost for my sake, he will find his true self."

Nobody is left in any doubt as to what following the king means! In John 15:18–21 he says,

> If the world hates you, it hated me first, as you know well. If you belong to the world, the world would love its own; but because you do not belong to the world, because I have chosen you out of the world, for that reason the world hates you. Remember what I said: "A servant is not greater than his master! As they persecuted me, they will persecute you; they will

follow your teaching as little as they have followed mine. It is on my account that they will treat you thus, because they do not know the One who sent me."

We ask the Lord why. "Why, Lord, must you and we save the world in this way? Why is it necessary to be spat upon and ridiculed and to suffer and to die before we can rise again with you?" Jesus always told his disciples that to suffer and to die was necessary. He never said a single word to explain why. So we look at him silently; we put aside the logic of reason and take on the logic of faith, the logic of the heart. We accept him on his own terms and say to him what Peter said, "Lord, I am ready to go with you to prison and to death."

But, being weak like Peter, we will ask for three graces:

1. The grace not to be deaf to his call.

Jesus calls us today, too, to follow him in suffering and death. It is very difficult to hear this call of his; we are past masters in the art of selective hearing; we hear only what suits us. What suffering, what kind of death is the Lord calling me to, today? Dietrich Bonhoeffer says somewhere that when Christ calls people he bids them come and die. So we must not be fooled when we hear Christ saying, "Come," to us. What he really means is, "Come and die."

2. The grace of understanding.

The grace of understanding is the grace of being able to think as God thinks, not as human beings think. This is a pure grace. No amount of intellectual effort on our part will give us the ability to think as God thinks. There is a wisdom of God that appears folly to humankind. I advise you to read the first three chapters of Paul's first letter to the Corinthians. They are full of this theme.

This doctrine of the cross is sheer folly to those on their way to ruin, but to us who are on the way to salvation it is the power of God. Scripture says, "I will destroy the wisdom of the wise, and bring to nothing the cleverness of the clever." God had made the wisdom of this world look foolish. As God in his wisdom ordained, the world failed to find him by its wisdom, and he chose to save those who have faith by the folly of the Gospel. Jews call for miracles, Greeks look for wisdom; but we proclaim Christ—yes, Christ nailed to the cross; and though this is a stumbling block to Jews and folly to Greeks, yet to those who have heard his call, Jews and Greeks alike, he is the power of God and the wisdom of God. Divine folly is wiser than the wisdom of man and divine weakness stronger than man's strength.

Even the apostles who lived so long with Christ did not fully grasp this teaching regarding his kingdom. To the very end, before his ascension, they ask him stupid questions that clearly show they have failed to grasp what he was teaching them so painstakingly. "Lord, is this the time when you are to establish once again the sovereignty of Israel?" they ask (Acts 1:6). To understand this they needed the Holy Spirit who came upon them at Pentecost. We, too, need the Spirit if we are to understand Christ's teaching. No one else can make us understand this, no retreat master, no book, not Christ himself, for even he failed completely with the apostles. So if we are to understand, we must ask for the gift of the Spirit.

> For the Spirit explores everything, even the depths of God's own nature . . . this is the Spirit that we have received from God, and not the spirit of the world, so that we may know all that God of his own grace gives us. . . . A man who is unspiritual refuses what belongs to the Spirit of God; it is folly to him; he cannot grasp it, because it needs to be judged in the light of the Spirit. A man gifted with the Spirit can judge the worth of everything, but is not himself subject to judgement by his fellow-men. For (in the words of Scripture) "Who knows the

mind of the Lord? Who can advise him?" We, however, possess the mind of Christ.

This is the Spirit we must ask for if we, too, are to have the mind of Christ and think the thoughts of God.

One way to grasp this teaching of Christ is to become a little child. When we become little children before God, he stoops down and makes us his confidants and he gives us a wisdom that our own thinking would never be able to produce.

> I thank thee, Father, Lord of heaven and earth, for hiding these things from the learned and wise, and revealing them to the simple. Yes, Father, such was thy choice.
>
> Matthew 11:25

3. The grace to follow him all our lives.

The third grace will mean much suffering, carrying the cross with Christ—not just hard work, but sharing in a destiny like his own. It is significant that when Paul is converted he says, "Lord, what do you want me to do?" (Acts 22:10). The Lord replies to that question in the words he says to Ananias: "This man is my chosen instrument, to carry my name among nations and their kings and among the children of Israel as well. I myself will show him how much he must suffer for my name." The world is not redeemed by doing, but by the cross. We adore thee, O Christ, and we bless thee, because by thy holy Cross thou hast redeemed the world! And so Paul would say later to his Philippians, "All I care for is to know Christ, to experience the power of his resurrection and to share his sufferings, in growing conformity with his death" (Philippians 3:10).

I shall point out to you in a later conference how following Christ in all the radicalism of the Gospels is going to mean hardships and poverty and being considered a fool. This is inevitable once you start thinking and judging the way God thinks and judges, and start talking and acting accordingly. I shall leave this for later. I only want to stress one point here, which I shall also dwell on later, namely, that the following of Christ, the carrying of his cross, leads not to sadness, but to joy and happiness. This is the Good News that Jesus brings us: the secret of happiness that humankind has been longing for, for centuries. This is not a gospel of gloom. It is only the superficial who think that happiness is not compatible with suffering, even much suffering that is undertaken out of love. Paul is a fine example of this. How much he suffered for Christ. He even speaks of bearing the marks of the dying Jesus on his body and of making up what is still wanting to the sufferings of Christ. And yet, what a joyous saint he was! A messenger of peace and joy that he obviously possessed in overflowing measure as we can see from his letters to his Christians. If we take a decision to follow Christ totally, it is a hard life we are opting for, but it is important that we realize that it is also a happy life. If we understand this, we shall follow him more readily and wholeheartedly and more perseveringly, comforted by his loving presence and the strength of his Holy Spirit.

15

To Know, to Love,
to Follow Christ

I have spoken to you about the kingship of Christ and about his call to us to follow him in carrying his cross. I invite you for the next few days to make this the theme of your prayer: discipleship, the following of Christ, carrying his cross. To follow him is not possible without our first coming to know and love him. And this is the grace I want you to ask God for these days: the grace to know Christ, to love Christ, to follow Christ faithfully. In this conference I should first like to say something about this knowing, loving, and following. Then I want to propose to you a method for praying over the life of Christ that might aid you in attaining the grace to know, to love, and to follow.

To Know Christ

To know Christ means to meet him. This is how we know a person. There's a difference between *knowing about* a person and *knowing* a person. The latter is only possible when we have met him or her personally. So ask for the grace of knowing Christ personally.

This is the kind of knowledge the good Samaritans had of Jesus after he was introduced to them by the Samaritan woman, in John 4.

Many Samaritans of that town came to believe in him because of the woman's testimony: "He told me everything I ever did." So when these Samaritans had come to him they pressed him to stay with them; and he stayed there two days. Many more became believers because of what they heard from his own lips. They told the woman, "It is no longer because of what you said that we believe, for we have heard him ourselves; and we know that this is in truth the Saviour of the World."

This is the aspiration of every priest, cathechist, and teacher of the Gospels: that our audience should say to us, "It is no longer because of what you have said that we believe, for we have seen and heard him ourselves." This is the kind of knowledge of Christ that I am speaking of. A knowledge that is imparted by Christ himself, not by books or preachers.

St. Paul treasured this knowledge so much that he was ready to exchange everything in the world for it. Listen to his moving words:

> All such assets I have written off because of Christ. I would say more: I count everything sheer loss, because all is far outweighed by the gain of knowing Christ Jesus my Lord, for whose sake I did in fact lose everything. I count it so much garbage, for the sake of gaining Christ and finding myself incorporate in him, with no righteousness of my own, no legal rectitude. . . . All I care for is to know Christ, to experience the power of his resurrection, and to share his sufferings, in growing conformity with his death.
>
> Philippians 3:7–10

Is the knowledge of Christ for us what it was for St. Paul? We are busy today picking up so many other types of knowledge for the sake of the apostolate, we say, and we are probably wise to do so. However, if we fail in attaining this knowledge, all the rest—all our degrees and studies—are a total waste. I remember reading once the comparison of a watchmaker who entered the army.

When it was discovered that he was good at repairing watches, he was given so much repair work that when the time came to fight he was just too busy with repairing watches to have any time for fighting—or even the knowledge or inclination to fight effectively. How many priests today have specialized in all sorts of disciplines, but know so little about Christ. They just don't have the time for it (what on earth are they so very busy about, one wonders), and they could hardly be expected to have a zest for giving to others what they themselves have failed to learn.

You must be quite convinced about one thing: this knowledge of Christ is something that no amount of reflection or meditation on your part will ever give you. This is a pure gift of God. All you can do is ask for it humbly and persistently in prayer. I suggest that you ask Our Lady to intercede for you and obtain this grace for you. It is the Father who must introduce you to Christ and show you who he is:

> Simon, son of Jonah, you are favoured indeed! You did not learn that from mortal man; it was revealed to you by my heavenly Father. . . . I thank thee, Father, Lord of heaven and earth, for hiding these things from the learned and wise, and revealing them to the simple. Yes, Father, such was thy choice. Everything is entrusted to me by my Father; and no one knows the Son but the Father and no one knows the Father but the Son and those to whom the Son may choose to reveal him.
>
> Matthew 16:17; 11:25–27

To attain this knowledge a person must be "given" to the Son by the Father.

> This is eternal life: to know thee who alone art truly God, and Jesus Christ whom thou hast sent. . . . I have made thy name

known to the men whom thou didst give me out of the
world.

John 17:3.6

All that the Father gives me will come to me, and the man
who comes to me I will never turn away. . . . It is his will that
I should not lose even one of all that he has given me. . . . No
man can come to me unless he is drawn by the Father who
sent me.

John 6:37ff.

I am the good shepherd; I know my own sheep and my sheep
know me.

John 10:14

The disciples attained this knowledge of Christ only gradually.
In John 14:9 we read, "Have I been all this time with you, Philip,
and you still do not know me?" And in Luke 9:44–45,

Jesus said to his disciples, "What I now say is for you: pon-
der my words. The Son of Man is going to be given up into
the power of men." But they did not understand what he
said; it had been hidden from them so that they should not
perceive its drift; and they were afraid to ask him what it
meant.

This matter of the knowledge of Christ being a pure gift of
God is expressed admirably, by as unlikely a person as Mahatma
Gandhi. You know what a great admirer he was of Jesus and how
heroically he put into practice in his life the principles of the Sermon on the Mount. Yet he never became a Christian, and could
not accept Jesus as the Son of God. The Protestant evangelist, Stan-
ley Jones, who was a great admirer of Gandhi, once wrote the following letter to him:

You know my love for you and how I've tried to interpret you and your non-violent movement to the West. But I am rather disappointed in one matter. I thought you had grasped the centre of the Christian faith, but I'm afraid I must change my mind. I think you have grasped certain principles of the Christian faith which have moulded you, and have helped make you great—you have grasped the principles, but you have missed the Person. You said in Calcutta to the missionaries that you did not turn to the Sermon on the Mount for consolation, but to the Bhagavad Gita. Neither do I turn to the Sermon on the Mount for consolation, but to this Person who embodies and illustrates the Sermon on the Mount; but he is much more. Here is where I think you are weakest in your grasp. May I suggest that you penetrate through the principles to the Person and then come back and tell us what you have found. I don't say this as a mere Christian propagandist. I say this because we need you and need the illustration you could give us if you really grasped the centre, the Person.

Gandhi replied immediately:

I appreciate the love underlying the letter and kind thought for my welfare, but my difficulty is of long standing. Other friends have pointed it out to me before now. I cannot grasp the position by the intellect; the heart must be touched. Saul became Paul not by an intellectual effort but by something touching his heart. All I can say is that my heart is absolutely open; I have no axes to grind. I want to find the truth, to see God face to face.

Let us then ask the Father to draw us to Christ and to give us the knowledge of Christ, since no one knows Christ except the Father. Let us ask the Holy Spirit for this grace, for the Spirit explores everything, even the depths of God's own nature. Among men, who knows what a man is but the man's own spirit within him? In the same way, only the Spirit of God knows what God is. This is the Spirit that we have received from God, and not the spirit of the world, so that we may know all that God of his own grace gives us.

1 Corinthians 2:10–12

To Love Christ

It is not possible to know Christ in the way I have described without falling in love with him and being captivated by his goodness and loveliness. The deeper our knowledge of him, the greater our love will be. And the more our love for him, the deeper will be our knowledge, for to really know a person it is important to see him through the eyes of love.

Jesus claimed this love for himself. Every religious reformer pointed to an ideal outside himself. Only Christ points to himself and makes himself the center of his teaching. Follow *me*, not just the doctrine or the ideal I propound. He who loves father or mother more than me is not worthy of me. I am the way, the truth, the life. In as much as you did it to the least of my brethren, you did it to me. When he goes to his hometown of Nazareth, it is himself he proclaims, and then he commands their loyalty and faith.

Unrolling the scroll he found the place where it is written: "The Spirit of the Lord has been given to me, for he has anointed me. . . . Then he began to speak to them, 'This text is being fulfilled today even as you listen.' "

Conversion is not just conversion to an intellectual system or philosophy or even a message from God; it is, ultimately, the turning of our heart totally to the Father. But it is also essentially a conversion to Christ. It is a conversion of the heart to Christ (*heart* in the biblical sense, meaning the center of one's personality, the seat of one's spirit, one's freedom, one's attachments). It is a heart turned toward Christ: the *metanoia;* a heart inhabited by Christ, filled with him ("May Christ find a dwelling place in your heart by faith" [Ephesians 3:17]); a heart assimilated to Christ, taking on his values and judgments and point of view regarding God, the world, life, humanity ("Let this mind be in you which was in Christ Jesus" [Philippians 2:5]; "Who knows the mind of the Lord? Who can advise him? We, however, possess the mind of Christ" [1 Corinthians 2:16]).

So let us not hesitate to give our whole heart to Christ, to pour all the wealth of our love and affection onto him. Let us strive to attain that fantastic love that Paul had, a love that was so strong that he could make the boldest claims.

> Then what can separate us from the love of Christ? Can affliction or hardship? Can persecution, hunger, nakedness, peril or the sword? I am convinced that there is nothing in death or life, in the realm of spirits or superhuman powers, in the world as it is or the world as it shall be, in the forces of the universe, in heights or depths—nothing in all creation that can separate us from the love of God in Christ Jesus our Lord.
>
> Romans 8:35–39

To Follow Christ

I have spoken sufficiently of following Christ in the previous conference. All I wish to do here is emphasize the fact that when we are called to follow Christ in carrying our cross, we are not being called to follow him in sadness and gloom. If it is true that no one on earth is so happy as those who have found God and given their hearts entirely to God, there is no doubt that Jesus Christ was the happiest person on earth. He told his disciples that it was necessary for the Messiah to suffer and thus to enter into his glory. And this is what he promises to us who follow him: if we follow him in suffering we shall follow him in glory. It is wrong to think, however, that the glory will only come after death. A large share of it is given to us right now on earth. Jesus tells us in the Sermon on the Mount that the poor, the meek, the peaceful, are truly lucky, happy. He is not talking of the happiness of heaven primarily. He is speaking of the happiness that we shall experience in the very living out of the beatitudes. The happiness that comes from the fruits—joy, peace, and love—of the Spirit, who is already given to us now (Galatians 5).

Isn't it significant that in the very discourse in which Jesus predicted that his apostles would be persecuted and would suffer, he promises them joy and peace? "I have told you all this to guard you against the breakdown of your faith. They will ban you from the synagogue: indeed, the time is coming when anyone who kills you will suppose that he is performing a religious duty," he says in John 16:1–2). But then he talks to them, in the same breath, so to speak, of the peace and the joy he will give them in the midst of their sufferings:

> Peace is my parting gift to you, my own peace, such as the world cannot give. Set your troubled hearts at rest, and banish your fears. . . . I have spoken thus to you, so that my joy may be in you, and your joy complete. . . . Are you discussing what I said: "A little while, and you will not see me, and again a little while, and you will see me?" In very truth I tell you, you will weep and mourn, but the world will be glad. But though you will be plunged in grief, your grief will be turned to joy. A woman in labour is in pain because her time has come; but when the child is born she forgets the anguish in her joy that a man has been born into the world. So it is with you: for the moment you are sad at heart; but I shall see you again, and then you will be joyful and no one shall rob you of your joy. Ask

and you will receive, that your joy may be complete. . . . I have told you all this so that in me you may find peace. In the world you will have trouble. But courage! The victory is mine; I have conquered the world.

John 14:27; 15:11; 16:19–24, 33

This prophecy of Jesus was fulfilled immediately after his death, both in the lives of the apostles and in those of the early Christians. In Acts 5:40 we read,

> They sent for the apostles and had them flogged; then they ordered them to give up speaking in the name of Jesus, and discharged them. So the apostles went out from the Council rejoicing that they had been found worthy to suffer indignity for the sake of the Name."

Acts 13:50–52 says,

> A persecution was started against Paul and Barnabas and they were expelled from the district . . . and the converts were filled with joy and with the Holy Spirit."

St. Paul says to his Thessalonians,

> The welcome you gave the message meant grave suffering for you, yet you rejoiced in the Holy Spirit.

St. Paul certainly experienced this mystery of joy and peace in the cross in his own life and he gives witness to it eloquently. I should like to share with you some passages from his letters where he describes what the following of Christ meant to him. He speaks, also, of the consolation that this brought him. You may want to take these passages to prayer and find inspiration in them:

Praise be to the God and Father of Our Lord Jesus Christ, the all-merciful Father, the God whose consolation never fails us! He comforts us in all our troubles so that we in turn may be able to comfort others in any trouble of theirs and share with them the consolation we ourselves receive from God. As Christ's cup of suffering overflows, and we suffer with him, so also through Christ our consolation overflows.

2 Corinthians 1:3–5

It makes me happy to suffer for you, as I am suffering now, and in my own body to do what I can to make up all that has still to be undergone by Christ for the sake of his body, the Church.

Colossians 1:25

The Jerusalem Bible's comment on this is: Jesus suffered in order to establish the reign of God and anyone who continues his work must share this suffering.

We prove we are servants of God by great fortitude in times of suffering; in times of hardship and distress; when we are flogged; or sent to prison, or mobbed; labouring, sleepless, starving. We prove we are God's servants by our purity, knowledge, patience and kindness; by a spirit of holiness, by a love free from affectation; by the world of truth and the power of God . . . prepared for honour or disgrace, for blame or praise; taken for imposters while we are genuine; obscure yet famous; said to be dying and here we are alive; rumoured to be executed before we are sentenced; thought most miserable and yet we are always rejoicing; taken for paupers though we make others rich, for people having nothing though we have everything.

2 Corinthians 6:3ff.

But if anyone wants some brazen speaking—I am still talking as a fool—then I can be as brazen as any of them, and about the same things. Hebrews are they? So am I. Israelites? So am I. Descendants of Abraham? So am I. The servants of Christ? I must be mad to say this, but so am I, and more than they; more because I have worked harder. I have been sent to prison more often, and whipped so many times harder. Five times I had the thirty-nine lashes from the Jews; three times I have been beaten with sticks; once I was stoned; three times I have been shipwrecked and once adrift in the open sea for a night and a day. Constantly travelling, I have been in danger from rivers and in danger from brigands, in danger from my own people and in danger from pagans; in danger in the towns, in danger in the open country, danger at sea and danger from so-called brothers. I have worked and laboured often without sleep; I have been hungry and thirsty and often starving; I have been in the cold without clothes. And, to leave out much more, there is my daily preoccupation; my anxiety for all the Churches. . . . Must I go on boasting, though there is nothing to be gained by it? But I will move on to the visions and revelations I have had from the Lord. I know a man in Christ, who, fourteen years ago, was caught up—whether still in the body or out of the body, I do not know; God knows—right into the third heaven. I do know, however, that this same person—whether in the body or out of the body, I do not know; God knows—was caught up into paradise and heard things which must not and cannot be put into human language. In view of the extraordinary nature of these revelations, to stop me from getting too proud I was given a thorn in the flesh, an angel of Satan to beat me and stop me from getting too proud! About this thing, I have pleaded with the Lord three times for it to leave me but he has said, "My grace is enough for you; my power is at its best in weakness." So I shall be very happy to make my weaknesses my special boast so that the power of Christ may stay over me, and that is why I am quite content with my weaknesses, and with insults, hardships, persecutions, and the agonies I go through for Christ's sake. For it is when I am weak that I am strong.

2 Corinthians 11:21ff.

Have you noticed the things that Paul the apostle boasts of? He put up no buildings; he made no headlines; he had no worldly success. He boasts of the hardships and sufferings he underwent for Christ and his mystical experiences and of his weakness, which give him the opportunity to experience Christ's power!

I have been crucified with Christ, and I live now not with my own life but with the life of Christ who lives in me. The life I now live in this body I live in faith; faith in the Son of God who loved me and who sacrificed himself for my sake.

Galatians 2:19

"I want no more trouble from anybody after this; the marks on my body are those of Jesus" (Galatians 6:17). The comment of the Jerusalem Bible on this passage is: The marks of ill-treatment suffered for Christ. Cf. 2 Corinthians 6:4–5, 11:23ff.

We are no better than pots of earthenware to contain this treasure, and this proves that such transcendent power does not come from us, but is God's alone. Hard-pressed on every side, we are never hemmed in; bewildered, we are never at our wits' end; hunted, we are never abandoned to our fate; struck down, we are not left to die. Wherever we go we carry death with us in our body, the death that Jesus died, that in this body also life may reveal itself, the life that Jesus lives. For continually, while still alive, we are being surrendered into the hands of death, for Jesus' sake, so that the life of Jesus also may be revealed in this mortal body of ours. . . . Indeed, it is for your sake that all things are ordered, so that, as the abounding grace of God is shared by more and more, the greater may be the chorus of thanksgiving that ascends to the glory of God. No wonder we do not lose heart! Though our outward humanity is in decay, yet day by day, we are inwardly renewed.

2 Corinthians 4:7ff.

My one hope and trust is that I shall never have to admit defeat, but that now as always I shall have the courage for Christ to be glorified in my body, whether by my life or by my death. Life to me, of course, is Christ, but then death would bring me something more; but then again, if living in this body means doing work which is having good results—I do not know what I should choose. I am caught in this dilemma: I want to be gone and be with Christ, which would be very much better; but for me to stay alive in this body is a more urgent need for your sake. This weighs with me so much that I feel sure I shall survive and stay with you all, and help you to progress in faith and even increase your joy in it; and so you will have another reason to give praise to Christ Jesus on my account when I am with you again.

Philippians 1:20ff.

To these passages you may add Philippians 3:7ff. and Romans 8:35ff., which I have quoted to you in previous conferences and so will not repeat here.

And here are some texts from the Gospels connected with the following of Christ:

He who loves father or mother more than me is not worthy of me; and he who loves son or daughter more than me is not worthy of me. And he who does not take up his cross and follow me, is not worthy of me. He who finds his life will lose it, and he who loses his life for my sake, will find it.

Matthew 10:37ff.; cf. 16:24–26

If anyone comes to me and does not hate his father and mother, and wife and children, and brothers and sisters, yes, and even his own life, he cannot be my disciple. And he who does not carry his cross and follow me cannot be my disciple. For which of you, wishing to build a tower, does not sit down first and calculate the outlays that are necessary, whether he has the means to complete it? Lest, after he has laid the foundation he is not able to finish all who behold begin to mock him. . . . So therefore, everyone of you who does not renounce all that he possesses, cannot be my disciple.

Luke 14:26–29, 33

If anyone would serve me, let him follow me; and where I am there also shall my servant be.

John 12:26

To the request of the sons of Zebedee for the first two places in the kingdom, Jesus replies: "You do not know what you are asking for. Can you drink of the cup of which I drink, or be baptized with the baptism with which I am to be baptized?" And they said to him, "We can." And, giving this instruction a more general hearing, he continues,

Whoever wishes to become great shall be your servant; and whoever wishes to be first among you shall be the slave of all; for the Son of Man also has not come to be served but to serve, and to give his life as a ransom for many.

Mark 10:38–39; 43–45

The hour has come for the Son of Man to be glorified. Amen I say to you, unless the grain of wheat fall into the ground and die it remains alone. But if it die it brings forth much fruit. He who loves his life loses it; and he who hates his life in this world keeps it unto life everlasting. If anyone would serve me, let him follow me; and where I am there also shall my servant be. If anyone serves me, my Father will honour him.

John 12:23ff.

Remember the word that I have spoken to you: No servant is greater than his master. If they have persecuted me they will persecute you also; if they have kept my word they will keep yours also.

John 15:20

As they were going along the road a man said to him, "I will follow you wherever you go." Jesus answered, "Foxes have their holes, the birds their roosts; but the Son of Man has nowhere to lay his head." To another he said, "Follow me," but the man replied, "Let me go and bury my father first." Jesus said, "Leave the dead to bury their dead; you must go and announce the kingdom of God." Yet another said, "I will follow you, sir; but let me first say goodbye to my people at home." To him Jesus said, "No one who sets his hand to the plough and then keeps looking back is fit for the kingdom of God."

Luke 9:57–62

Take one or other of these passages to prayer if you wish, as means for drawing inspiration to follow Christ more faithfully. But above all, ask persistently for this grace. Persistent prayer and faith will bring you what much meditation and reflection will not. I told you I would offer you a method of contemplation on the life of Christ that may help you to come to know and love Christ more deeply. But I shall leave this for the next conference.

16

Meditation on the Life of Christ

There is a form of meditation on the life of Christ as it is given in the Gospels that is highly recommended by a number of saints as being very helpful for achieving intimacy with Christ. It involves the use of fantasy. Fantasy is a tool that many modern psychotherapists are using to very good effect. They are beginning to realize that the world of fantasy is not quite as "unreal" as it seems to be, that far from being a world of escape and unreality it reveals realities as deep or even deeper than those grasped by our mind and so is a very effective tool for healing and growth.

I shall first describe this form of prayer and then comment on some of the difficulties that are brought against it. Take any scene from the life of Christ. I shall choose John 5:1–9 as an example that you can then apply to other scenes from the life of Christ.

> Later on Jesus went up to Jerusalem for one of the Jewish festivals. Now at the Sheep Pool in Jerusalem there is a place with five colonnades. Its name in the language of the Jews is Bethesda. In these colonnades there lay a crowd of sick people, blind, lame and paralysed (waiting for the disturbance of the water; for from time to time an angel came down into the pool and stirred up the water. The first to plunge in after this dis-

turbance recovered from whatever disease had afflicted him). Among them was a man who had been crippled for thirty-eight years. When Jesus saw him lying there and was aware that he had been ill a long time, he asked him, "Do you want to recover?" "Sir," he replied "I have no one to put me in the pool when the water is disturbed, but while I am moving, someone else is in the pool before me." Jesus answered, "Rise to your feet, take up your bed and walk." The man recovered instantly, took up his stretcher, and began to walk.

I want you now to go in fantasy to this place with five colonnades called Bethesda. See the sick people lying there. Move about among them. What do you feel as you see them there? At some distance you notice the crippled man. Walk up to him and speak with him. What do you think is the cause of his ailment? What kind of an impression does he make upon you? Do you like him or dislike him? While you are talking with him, you notice Jesus entering the place. He is looking around at the sick people. What do you think he is thinking and feeling? Does he stop to talk with any of them or does he come straight toward the crippled man? Move aside to make way for Jesus as he comes up and listen to what he says to the crippled man and to what the crippled man says to him. Don't miss any detail of Jesus' attitude, his feelings, his words, his behavior. Listen especially to those words of his, "Do you want to recover?" The Gospels give us only a fragment of Jesus's conversation. Fill it in with your imagination. Now listen to those powerful words of his, "Rise to your feet, take up your bed and walk." Notice what happens. The feelings and reactions of the crippled man, the feelings and reactions of Jesus.

Jesus now turns to you. Is there any illness that you are suffering from, physical, emotional, or spiritual? Talk to him about it and listen to what he has to say. What do you answer when he says to you, "Do you want to recover? Do you really want to recover, with all the consequences that recovery will bring? Many people do not want to recover because recovery brings pain with it or responsibility, or the giving up of something we want to hold on to." If your answer is, "Yes, Lord, I want to recover," then hear the Lord say his powerful word to you too. This is a moment of grace. Jesus is as real and as powerful and as present here and now as he was when he stood before that crippled man twenty centuries ago. If you have faith in his power you will experience his healing touch, less sensationally, perhaps, than the crippled man, but no less effectively. After this, spend some time in loving converse with him.

Now come the objections to this form of meditation. It doesn't matter that it has been recommended by mystics like St. Bonaventure and St. Ignatius of Loyola. The fact is that those scenes are simply not true. They are all made up. The answer to this is quite simple. The scene is obviously not true historically. It contains a truth, not of history, but of mystery. Let me explain that a little. St. Ignatius of Loyola, who recommends this method as the principle way of praying in his Spiritual Exercises, was a man who soon after his conversion made a pilgrimage to the Holy Land. He had read in the book of Ludolph of Saxony these words taken from Bonaventure:

> If you wish to draw profit from these meditations, set aside all cares and anxieties. Lovingly and contemplatively, with all the feelings of your heart, make everything that the Lord Jesus said and did present to yourself, just as though you were hearing it with your ears and seeing it with your eyes. And then all that will become sweet to you, because you are reflecting upon it with longing and savoring it yet more. And even when it is related in the past tense you should contemplate it all as though present today. Go into the Holy Land, kiss with fervent spirit the earth on which the good Jesus stood. Make present to yourself how he spoke and went about with his disciples, with

sinners; how he speaks and preaches, how he walks and rests, sleeps and wakes, eats and performs miracles. Write down in your heart his demeanor and his actions.

And, having read these words, he no doubt put them into practice in his prayer. But his ardent heart would not rest until he had seen the Holy Land for himself. Once there, he engraved every single detail in his memory, the hills and valleys and countryside that Jesus saw, roads he traveled, and houses he was reported to have lived in. On the Mount of Olives he piously venerated the rock from which Jesus was supposed to have ascended into heaven and on which his footprints were supposed to have been stamped. After leaving the mount, he suddenly realized that he hadn't noticed in what direction Jesus' feet were pointing when he ascended. So he went back on his own, a risky thing to do, and bribed the moorish guard there with the last possession of value he had, a penknife, for the privilege of noticing even this little detail. Now this same man, when writing his Spiritual Exercises, tells retreatants to reconstruct for themselves the scenes of the life of Christ. In his meditation on the Nativity he bids the retreatant "see in imagination the way from Nazareth to Bethlehem. Consider its length, its breadth; whether level, or through valleys and over hills. Observe also the place or cave where Christ is born; whether big or little; whether high or low; and how it is arranged." Why does he leave all this to retreatants' imaginations? He himself had seen these places (or what he piously believed to be these places), so could he not have given an accurate description of them? The fact of the matter is that it had little importance to reconstruct the scene with historical accuracy; in fact, it had no importance at all. Ignatius wants retreatants to go to their own fantasy Nazareth and their own fantasy Bethlehem. The fantasy will help bring out the truth of mystery, which is far more important than the truth of history. The fantasy will put us in touch with Jesus Christ. And this is much more important than all the historical accuracy in the world. St.

Francis of Assisi, we are told, went to Mount Alvernia where he had a vision of Jesus on the cross, and he lovingly took him down from the cross. Now St. Francis of Assisi was no fool; he was quite aware, at least as aware as we are today, that Jesus, having once died, dies no more. And yet, while he lovingly took him down from the cross and stood by him in his suffering, a deep mystery of love was being enacted, fantasy notwithstanding, before which the rational mind and rational theology must stop in silent incomprehension. It is to Francis, in fact, that we owe the beautiful custom of constructing cribs at Christmas time. Were he acquainted with the findings of modern scripture scholarship regarding the infancy narratives, I feel quite sure he would have gone right ahead and constructed his cribs all the same. Where the event took place historically just as it is narrated in the gospel text is simply beside the point. The point is that through these fantasy symbols, we come in touch with reality. If we will allow ourselves to become children again and plunge wholeheartedly into this world seemingly of make-believe, we might be delightfully surprised to discover Christ there behind all the fantasy and discover him in greater depth here than in all our theological reflection and speculation. St. Anthony of Padua is one of the many saints who are said to have held the Infant Jesus in their arms and regaled themselves with his loving caresses. St. Anthony, in addition to being no fool himself, was theologian enough to have been declared a Doctor of the Church, and should have surely known that Jesus is no longer an infant! He was also, fortunately, mystic enough to sense the deep mystical reality behind that vision of his and to surrender completely to the "fantasy reality," if I may use that expression, of the vision. If you, too, can become a child and enter this world of fantasy while you meditate on the Gospels you will probably discover many lovely hidden treasures that you will not discover in any other way. Spend a day with the Holy Family at Nazareth, for instance. Share their simple life, help them in their work, speak to Jesus and Mary and Joseph about their lives and their problems and about your own. Or join the disciples while the Lord instructs them in private and ask him questions of your own. Go to the house of Martha and Mary, and sit lovingly beside Mary while the Lord speaks or help poor distracted Martha with her household chores. You won't come away with any scriptural erudition. But the Lord will give you the hidden wisdom he has reserved for little children!

There is another objection to this method of prayer, quite apart from the historical difficulties involved in imagining things that took place long ago, and seeing them as if they were happening now. The objection could be stated thus: When I imagine Christ with me or before me and I talk to him, there's no problem there; the problem arises when I hear Christ talking back to me. That isn't Christ at all who is talking to me. It is the effect of my own imagination; it is I who am putting those words into his mouth. It is I, in effect, who am talking to myself.

This is true. Very often, chiefly when we first begin to practice this form of dialoguing with Christ, there is no more there than our own pious reflections that come to us in the form of Christ's words. That is what thinking or reflecting is: I talking to myself. Right now I am doing this through the image of Christ whom I imagine is present in front of me. It won't be long however, before you will sometimes notice that those words you imagine you hear as coming from Christ are no mere invention of your imagination. Sometimes the response itself will startle you, and you will wonder from where it came. It brings a great insight with it. At other times the words will seem very ordinary; no special light or insight will come with them. But the effect of these ordinary words is quite unusual: they bring a sudden and unexpected peace, great strength, intense consolation, or intense joy in God's service. Together with these feelings comes a conviction that somehow the Lord has communicated with you and made a gift to you under the cover of those words that you were "making" him say to you in your imagination.

Connected with this is a form of being aware of God's presence, of the presence of Christ with us throughout the day. It is much recommended by St. Teresa of Avila among others. It consists in imagining that Christ is by your side all day and they are in constant loving conversation with him. One author calls this the exercise of imaginative faith. A good expression. Imagine that Christ is sitting there on an empty chair in your room and speak with him just as you would if you actually saw him. This is not pure fantasy because what you are imagining is really there—Christ the Risen Lord—but he isn't there in the way you are imagining him, with the features and garments you are putting onto him.

This is more or less what St. Ignatius of Loyola recommends in his Spiritual Exercises when he says that the colloquy,

> is made by speaking exactly as one friend speaks to another, or as a servant speaks to a master, now asking him for a favour, now blaming himself for some misdeed, now making known his affairs to him, and seeking advice in them.

In another place Ignatius says,

> Imagine Christ our Lord present before you upon the cross, and begin to speak with him, asking how it is that though he is the Creator, he has stooped to become man, and to pass from eternal life to death here in time, that thus he might die for our sins.

Notice, incidentally, that he bids us ask Christ questions, ask him for advice, both of which presuppose some sort of answer from the Lord. Ignatius himself had no doubt about the fact that the Lord answers retreatants, revealing his will to them and guiding them personally, whether it be under the cover of imaginative faith or through a deep interior communication that is beyond all words and concepts and images. These are his words:

The retreat master ought not to urge the retreatant more to poverty or any promise than to the contrary, nor to one state of life or way of living more than to another. Outside the Exercises, it is true, we may lawfully and meritoriously urge all who probably have the required fitness to choose continence, virginity, the religious life, and every form of religious perfections. But while one is engaged in the Spiritual Exercises, it is more suitable and much better that *the Creator and Lord in person communicate himself to the devout soul* in quest of the divine will, that he inflame it with his love and praise, and dispose it for the way in which it could better serve God in future. Therefore, the retreat director, as a balance at equilibrium, without leaning to one side or the other, should *permit the Creator to deal directly with the creature*, and the creature directly with his Creator and Lord.

I shall have occasion to speak later of this interior communication between Creator and creature—what it means and how it takes place. For the time being suffice it to know, chiefly for those of us who know of no other way of "listening" to God and getting his guidance, that the Lord graciously speaks to us under the species of what I have called above imaginative faith. It is very hard to discern, with the mind, where imagination ends and reality begins. Become a little child, deal with God in simplicity of heart, and you will develop an instinct to discern the difference between pure imagination and reality, or rather, "Reality," with a capital "R," communicating with us through these images and fantasies.

I want to end this section with the words of a famous Hindu guru to whom a Catholic sister said, "You have said in the past that if any Christians became your disciples you would not seek to make them Hindu but you would try to make them better Christians. May I ask how you would go about doing this?" The good Hindu guru gave the sister a reply worthy of an excellent Catholic spiritual director. He suggested two of the first ways for coming to the experience of Jesus Christ the Risen Lord. He said, "I would strive to put them in touch with Jesus Christ. And I would get them to do this through keeping Christ constantly at their sides all through the day and through an assiduous reading of the Scriptures."

The Healing of Memories

As a kind of footnote to what I have said about meditating on the life of Christ through fantasy I should like to speak of the use of this method as a means of meditation on our own life with the purpose of experiencing healing and growth. Let me explain.

When I meditate on any scene in Christ's life, I make myself present to it. I imagine I am there, taking part in all the events, speaking, listening, acting. When I return to some scene in my past life, I relive it just as it happened with one difference: this time I get Christ to take an active part in it. Let me give you an example.

Suppose I return to a scene that causes me much distress. An event that brought me humiliation, like a public rebuke, or one that brought me great pain, like the death of a friend. I relive the whole event, in all its painful detail. I feel once more the pain, the loss, the humiliation, the bitterness. This time, however, Jesus is there. What role is he playing? Is he a comforter and strengthener? Is he the one who is causing me this pain and loss? I interact with him, just as I did with the other persons in that event. I seek strength from him, an explanation of what I don't understand; I seek a meaning to the whole event.

What is the purpose of this exercise? It is what some people call the healing of memories. There are memories that keep rankling within us—situations in our past life that have remained unresolved and continue to stir within us. This constitutes a perpetual wound that in some ways hampers us from plunging more fully into life, that sometimes seriously handicaps us in our ability to cope with life. Children who lose their mothers at an early age may decide, semiconsciously, never to love anyone again; all their lives they keep hankering after this mother-love that they will never get. Children who have lived in a situation of great fear or loneliness are constantly if unconsciously affected by this situation in the way they cope with life. Those who have been deeply humiliated by someone feel crippled in their self-respect or invest a considerable amount of emotional energy in desires to avenge themselves.

It is important for our personal growth, both spiritual and emotional, that we resolve these unresolved situations that keep rankling within us. When we relive them in the company of Christ, again and again, if need be, we will notice that a new meaning comes into them, that the sting goes out of them, that we can now return to them without any emotional upset; in fact, that we can even return to them now with a sense of gratitude to God, who planned these events for some purpose that will rebound to our benefit and to his glory. This form of prayer is good therapy and good spirituality.

What sort of events should we return to in our meditation? Events whose memory arouses within us "negative" emotions like the ones I mentioned before: pain, humiliation, feelings of inadequacy, grief, inferiority feelings, fear, etc. I recommend that you continue to return to these events as long as the negative feelings persist. When they die out, and you can even come to a point where you feel love and gratitude and a sense of praise for the event, there is no longer any need to return. The unresolved situation has been resolved and healed and even sanctified by the presence of Christ.

For many people it is even more important to return to another type of situation: events where they experienced intense joy or fulfillment or love and intimacy. These are the events that nourish and strengthen us, give us an infusion of fresh vitality and the desire to live life fully. Returning to them periodically and reliving them in all their pleasant detail brings us much psychological vigor and health. Reliving them in the presence of Christ brings us a spirit of gratitude and praise and a sense of God's goodness. It deepens our love for him and helps us grow in the spirit. There are hundreds of such events in our life that are rich in spiritual and emotional potential but that we discard and waste because we are too busy with the humdrum and drab details of daily living. A conversation with a friend, a picnic, an enjoyable party, a solitary walk by a lake or the sea, the embrace of a loved person, the joy and relief of good news, and scores of other situations.

If during this retreat there is some event in your past life that keeps coming up to distract you, claiming your attention because of the strong emotions involved—whether they be positive emotions like strong attachment and deep joy, or negative emotions like jealousy, frustration, bitterness, resentment—I recommend that you give some time each day to that situation, that you make a "meditation" out of it in the way I have indicated to you, and that you keep doing this until it gradually lapses into the background and ceases to distract you.

Appendix
Aids to Prayer

I want to share with you in this conference some tips on prayer that have proved very helpful to many people and are likely to be of help to a number of you too. It has often been said, and rightly, that prayer is something that comes naturally to human beings. Deep down the human being is a praying animal. But just because that is true, and it is, indeed, I would not have you think that prayer is something that is easy or something that does not need to be learned. It is natural for human beings to walk. But it takes a lot of learning for children to stand on their two legs and move—a lot of painful learning. It is also natural for human beings to love: yet how few are they who master the art of loving. This too, takes a lot of learning. And so it is with prayer. If we can accept the notion that prayer is an art and that, like most other arts, it calls for painful learning and much, much practice if one is to become proficient in it, then I think we will have taken a big step forward toward learning that art and, eventually, excelling in it.

Now the tips I am going to share with you will not be of equal value for each and every one of you. Some of you will find some of them quite useless, indeed, even distracting and harmful. If this is so, then do not scruple to discard them. They are meant to help you to pray, to make prayer easier and simpler and more effective, not to complicate things for you or make you more tense.

Having cleared the ground with those preliminary remarks I shall begin with a general statement that runs something like this: The principal reason why most people make little progress in the art of prayer is that they neglect to give their prayer all the human dimensions it needs.

Let me explain that. We are human beings, creatures of time and space. Creatures that have bodies and use words and live in communities and are swayed by emotions. Our prayer too must contain these elements. We need words when we pray. We need to pray with our bodies. We need time for prayer and a place that is appropriate. I am not offering this as a general rule, mind you. What I am saying is that, ordinarily speaking, our prayer is in need of all of the above, when it is at its early stages, when it is a tender growing plant. It will, in all likelihood, need them even when it has developed into a full-grown tree. But by then it will have developed an identity of its own and will be able to pick and choose from among these elements. In this conference I plan to speak of each of these elements: place, time, the body, words, music, sound, rhythm, community, and the emotions. Let us begin with the body.

The Body in Prayer

There is an author who speaks of a man whom he found sitting slouched in his armchair, smoking a cigarette. Said the author to the man, "You seem to be immersed in thought." The man replied, "I am praying." Said the author, "Praying? Tell me, if the Risen Lord were standing here in all his splendor and radiance, would you be sitting like that?" "No," said the man, "I imagine I wouldn't." "Then," said the author, "you do not at the moment have a consciousness of his presence here with you. You are not praying."

There is much truth in what that author said. Try it for yourself. On a day when you feel spiritually dry or tepid try to evoke the image of Jesus Christ standing before you in all the splendor of his resurrection. Then stand or sit or kneel before him with your hands devoutly joined in prayer before you. In other words, express, with your body, the sentiment of reverence and devotion that you would like to feel in his presence but do not now feel. You will, in all probability, notice that in a short while your heart and mind are also expressing what your body is expressing. Your awareness of his presence will be heightened and your sluggish heart will begin to warm. This is the great advantage of praying with your body, of taking your body along with you to pray. Many modern people insist that they are creatures of flesh and blood and body: they will say to you, "I do not just have a body, I am my body." They say that until they go to pray. Then it is as if they are pure spirit or pure mind; the body is just left out.

Nonverbal Communication

Many psychologists are aware of the value of saying things with one's body rather than with words. Here is something that I have tried in a therapy group. I will sometimes get members to communicate with others in the group only with their eyes—"Say something to your neighbor with your eyes"—or only with their hands. The force of communication achieved is nearly always evident. Sometimes they will say, "I cannot do it." They are afraid of looking ridiculous, they will say. Often it is not the ridiculousness that holds them back, it is the depth and genuineness of the communication involved—a depth and genuineness that they are not accustomed to and cannot sustain. Words are a more comfortable medium of expression—we can hide behind them, we can use them (as we generally do) not to communicate but to prevent true communication.

Sometimes I say to a group, "We shall spend the first ten minutes of this session communicating without words. Use any means you wish to communicate with others except words." Here again is an invitation to communicate with one's body, with eyes and hands and movements. Most people refuse to accept the invitation. They find it too threatening. The force and the truth of the communication is unbearable.

Try this when you next pray in your room. Stand before an image of Jesus Christ. Or just imagine him standing before you. Now look at him in a way that denotes supplication. Stay with that look for a while and notice what you feel. Then change the look to one of love or trust or joyful praise or sorrow and repentance or surrender. Try to express these dispositions or others only with your eyes. It might do a world of good to the intimacy and the depth of your communication with the Lord.

Or try expressing things to him with your body alone. Make a whole rite out of it. Stand alone in his presence for a while. Then slowly raise your head till your eyes are looking up to the ceiling. Hold that position for a while. Then gently raise both your hands, palms facing upwards, till they are on a level with your chest. Stop them there for a moment. Then bring them together smoothly and gently till both hands are touching each other and both palms face upwards, as if supporting a plate. (Or they can be drawn in to form a cup or chalice.) This posture is meant to express offering of oneself to God. Stay with this posture for three or four minutes, then slowly lower your head and hands. You may then either express this same disposition of offering again, going through this same rite (or possibly inventing another) or move on to express another attitude or disposition.

Here is one more: Stand erect in the middle of the room. Let your eyes look straight ahead of you, as if they were looking into the horizon. Then gently raise your hands till they come to the level of your chest and then move them outwards, till your arms are stretched wide apart, your palms facing outward. Hold this posture for three or four minutes. You may use it to express a longing and desire for the coming of the Lord. Or to express an attitude of welcome—to Him or to all people who are your brothers and sisters and whom you welcome into your heart.

One final example: stand for a moment in the presence of the Lord. Then kneel. Then join your hands in prayer in front of your chest. Stay like this for a while. Then slowly, very slowly, go down on all fours. You are like a beast of burden before the Lord. Go even further down now, till you are lying flat on the floor and let your arms move out till your whole figure forms a cross. Stay like this for a few minutes to express prostration or supplication or helplessness.

Do not limit yourselves to the examples I have given you. Be creative and invent your own way of expressing adoration or tenderness or sorrow or whatever, nonverbally, and you will discover the value of praying with your body. Centuries ago St. Augustine remarked that for some mysterious reason, he knew not which, every time he would lift his hands in prayer his heart would, after a while, be lifted up too and move toward God. I am reminded now that is exactly what the priest does at mass when he says, "Lift up your hearts"; he raises his arms upwards. It is a pity that we do not have the custom of lifting our arms too while we reply, "We have lifted them up to the Lord."

A Still Body

What I have suggested till now will prove a help if you wish to use your body actively in prayer; in other words, if you wish to actively pray with your body. It will prove a help for the times when you are engaged in what might be called devotional prayer.

There is, however, another form of prayer, many other forms, in fact—the prayer of quiet and stillness, prayer of fantasy and mind forms—in which movement of the body would impede rather than help. Then what is needed is perfect stillness of the body, a stillness that will foster peace and help dispel distractions. To achieve this stillness I suggest the following:

Sit down in a comfortable position, without slouching, however, and place your hands on your lap. Then become aware of various sensations that I am going to mention now, sensations that you have, but of which you are not explicitly aware. Become aware of the feel of your clothes on your shoulders. After three or four seconds move on to the awareness of the touch of your clothes on your back, or of your back touching the chair. Then the feel of your hands resting on your lap. Then the feel of your thighs pressing against the chair. Then the feel of the soles of your feet touching your shoes. Then become aware of your sitting posture. Then once again go the round of your shoulders, your back, your hands, your thighs, your feet, your hands. Do not dwell for more than three or four seconds on any one of these sensations.

After a while you may move to sensations in other parts of your body. The important thing to keep in mind is that you *feel* these sensations, not *think* them. A vast number of people have no feeling whatsoever in various parts of their body, or of any part of their body. All they have is a kind of mental map of their body. In doing this exercise, then, they are likely to move from one picture or image (of their hands, feet, back) to another rather than from one feeling to another or one sensation to another.

If you keep up this exercise for a while you will notice that your body is becoming relaxed. If you become tense, be aware of each of the tensions you are feeling. Notice where you are feeling tense, what kind of tension it is; in other words, how you are tensing yourself in that area. This too will gradually bring about a greater physical relaxation. There is another thing that will happen: your body will become perfectly still. Stay with that stillness for some time. Savor it, rest in it. Do not move in the slightest degree no matter how strong the urge to shift or fidget or scratch. If the urge to move becomes strong, become aware of the urge, of the impulse itself, and after a while it will quieten down and you will once again experience great bodily stillness. This stillness is an excellent setting for prayer. Now move on to prayer.

Bodily stillness will not, of course, take care of all the difficulties you are still going to have in prayer. Chief among these are distractions of the mind. There is something, however, that your body can do to help you cope with those distractions.

Those who are familiar with the practice of yoga tell us that when they achieve the lotus posture they frequently experience a perfect stillness, not only of body, but of mind as well. Some go so far as to say that in that posture it is impossible for them to think. The mind goes blank and they can only contemplate, not think. That is how influential the body can be on the state of our mind. The lotus posture, however, is not something that can be acquired without much pain and months of discipline, something that is ruled out for most of us. But even without the lotus posture there is much that your body can do for helping you cope with distractions.

One of the things you can do, if it helps you, is keep your eyes slightly open and fixed on a spot about three or four feet away from you. Many people find this a great help. When they close their eyes they somehow seem to set up a blank screen on which their mind then cheerfully proceeds to project all sorts of thoughts and images. Keeping their eyes half opened helps them to concentrate. It is important, of course, that their eyes not wander or that they not settle on a moving object, else this will be a new source of distraction. If you find that keeping your eyes open is a help to prayer, then fix them on an object or on some spot a little distance away from you and plunge into prayer. One last precaution: make sure you do not rest your eyes on any luminous object. This is likely to produce a mild form of hypnosis.

Another thing you can do is keep your back straight. It is a mysterious thing that a curved spine seems to foster distractions while a spine that is erect seems to keep them away. I am told that some Zen masters are able to tell whether students of theirs are distracted or not by merely looking at the straightness or curvature of their backs. Now I am not sure that a curved back necessarily indicates a distracted mind. I have sometimes prayed without distractions even when my back was not erect. But I do believe that a straight back is a great help for quietening the mind. In fact, there are some Tibetan monks who give so much importance to a straight back as an aid to meditation that they recommend meditators lie flat on their backs while meditating. A good enough recommendation, except for the fact that most people I know tend to fall asleep a few minutes after they have straightened their backs in this way!

The Problem of Tension and Restlessness

Many modern people are, unfortunately, quite incapable of sitting still. They are so restless and tense that even a minute or two of sitting still tends to increase their tension. And yet, it is important for prayer that we be able to be physically still. There is no doubt, of course, that prayer can go on while one is moving, and it frequently does. Ordinarily, however, it is not deep prayer. As soon as a moment of deep prayer descends upon those who are pacing up and down, they tend to stand still, as if caught up in something, immersed in something. There are deep mystical experiences that come upon people that make them want to jump and dance and move about, true; but these are the exception rather than the rule. Ordinarily deep prayer requires a still body—or it produces one. And so I do not recommend that you pace up and down while you are praying. Try the following if the urge to move is very great:

Become aware of the urge, the impulse that you experience. Notice the physical effects of this in your body, the tension, the area where you feel the tension, your resistance to the urge, the impulse. If after a few minutes you have still not quietened down, then pace up and down in your room very slowly, in the following fashion:

move your right leg forward and be fully aware of the sensation of movement in your right foot being lifted, then of its being thrust forward, then of its resting on the ground, then of the weight of the body leaning on it. Then do the same with your left foot. It might help you to concentrate if you interiorly verbalize what is happening, thus: "Right foot lifting. Right foot moving. Right foot rest. Right foot firm. Left foot lifting. Left foot moving. Left foot resting. Left foot firm . . ." This will help enormously to quiet your bodily tensions and your compulsion to move. Then stay in one posture for a while and see if you can hold it long enough to pray.

If you happen to be so tense and restless that even this does not help, then I suggest that you pace up and down in your room or in a quiet corner of a garden. This may alleviate your tension. Make sure that while you pace up and down your eyes do not take a stroll too, or that will be the ruin of your concentration and your prayer. Keep in mind, however, that this is only a temporary concession to your restlessness and continue every now and then to return to a stationary posture and to accustom your body to being still.

There is something else you might do if you simply have to move. Pray with your body as I suggested before, moving it in slow, peaceful gestures. Or change your posture every three or four minutes—very slowly, however, without jerks. Remember the petals of the flower opening. It may well happen that after a while you will rest in one of these postures and there will be no need for change.

Your Favorite Posture

If you develop some experience in prayer it will not be long before you find one posture that suits you best at prayer, and you will almost invariably assume this posture each time you pray. Experience will also teach you the wisdom of holding on to this posture and not changing it too easily. It seems strange that one would be able to love God better or get in touch with God more easily by means of one posture rather than another, but this is precisely what a famous English mystic, Richard Rolle, tells us.

Whatever the posture you find best suited to your own prayer, whether it be kneeling or standing or sitting or lying prostrate, I recommend that you not change it too easily—even if it seems at first slightly painful. Bear with the pain; the fruit you derive from prayer will be well worth it. Only if the pain becomes so strong as to be distracting should you change your posture. And then do so gently, very slowly, "like the petals of a flower gradually opening up or closing," to quote an Indian spiritual writer.

The ideal posture will be one that combines respect for the presence of God with repose and peace of the body. Much practice will give you this peace and stillness and respect, and then you will find in your body a valuable ally to your prayer and, on occasion, even a positive stimulus to prayer.

The Fragility of Our Prayer Life

Some people become disturbed at so much talk about "aids" to our prayer life. Is our prayer life something that needs to be tended and protected and cared for and fussed over? Isn't it overdoing it considerably to be so turned in on ourselves, to watch over our prayer life and hem it in with all sorts of protective devices?

It is. But the fact of the matter is that our prayer life, like all life on this planet, is very fragile, and the sooner we come to the realization of this truth the better. How carefully Nature has surrounded us with all sorts of helps to life without which we would not survive. Let the pressure of the atmosphere increase or decrease beyond a certain point, let the temperature become exceedingly hot or cold, and life—animal, plant, and human—is instantly snuffed out. We need to eat and drink daily and to draw air into our lungs each minute if we are to survive. And what great pains medical science takes to protect our health and physical well-being.

Thanks to all these precautions, human beings can live longer nowadays, and more healthily.

It isn't as if our prayer life is always going to need all these aids and props. A time will come when the tender sapling will grow into a robust oak tree and will be able to withstand the buffeting of the winds of life, even to thrive on them. But till that growth occurs we would do well to protect it, shelter it, and nourish it constantly. Perhaps our own experience will have shown us how easily our prayer life suffers or even perishes when we omit to surround it with recollection, with silence, spiritual reading, and a host of other helps that seem cumbersome after a while to those who are impatient for results and seek fruit from trees they haven't painstakingly cultivated.

Choosing a Place for Prayer

One frequently ignored aid to prayer is place. The place you choose to pray in can affect your prayer very considerably for good or evil. Has it ever struck you that Jesus would choose his places for prayer? If there was anyone who did not need to do this it would have been he, for he was the Master of Prayer, constantly in touch with his Heavenly Father. And yet he will take all the trouble to climb a mountain when he decides to spend a longer time in prayer. That seems to have been his favorite place for prayer, the mountaintop; he goes to a mountaintop to pray before the Sermon on the Mount, when the crowd seeks to make him king, on the day of his transfiguration. Or he goes to the garden of Gethsemane, which also seems to have been a praying place of his. Or he goes to what the Gospels call a desert place. He withdraws and chooses a place that is conducive to prayer.

There are some places that seem to foster prayer. The quiet of a garden, the shady bank of a flowing river, the peace of a mountain, the infinite expanse of the sea, the terrace exposed to the stars in the night or to the loveliness of dawn, the morning star, the rising sun; the sacred darkness of a dimly lit church—all of these seem almost to produce prayer within us when we put ourselves into them.

We shall not always have the luxury of living in places like these, of course—chiefly those of us who are condemned to live in gigantic modern cities—but once we have exposed ourselves to them we can carry them around with us in our hearts. Then it is enough for us to go back to them even in imagination in order to derive all the prayer benefits that we got from actually being in them. Even pictures of these places can be a help to prayer. There is a very prayerful and holy Jesuit I know who has a small collection of the lovely scenes of nature that one finds in modern calendars. He told me that when he is tired he just gazes for a while at one of those pictures and finds he is immersed in prayer. Father Teilhard speaks somewhere of the "spiritual potential of matter." Matter is indeed charged with spirit and this is rarely more evident than in these "prayerful places," if we will only learn to draw on all the prayer potential with which they are charged.

We must beware of a kind of "angelism" that leads us to think that we are above all these helps that "holy" places or beautiful places can offer us for prayer. It takes humility to accept our own immersion in matter and our dependence on matter even for our spiritual needs. I remember a Jesuit priest saying to us, when I was a seminarian, "The mistake we Jesuits make in helping lay people to pray is to imagine that because we need no helps to pray, they don't either. Lay people need the help that a prayerful atmosphere offers to prayer—the atmosphere of a church with statues and pictures that remind one of God. Now with us Jesuits it is different because of our intellectual formation. We can stop work at our desk and plunge into prayer right there, surrounded by our books and papers and our workaday atmosphere." Now that I have some considerable experience in directing Jesuits in prayer and the spiritual life, I am pretty much convinced that this good priest was right in what he said about our lay people and wrong in what he said about his fellow Jesuits who, being human beings after all, are just as much in need of a prayerful place and prayerful atmosphere when they go to pray as are laypersons—more so, in fact, because of their sometimes overly intellectual formation.

In his Spiritual Exercises St. Ignatius recommends that to better obtain the spiritual fruit that the retreatants are seeking during the first week of the exercises, in other words, to better obtain the grace of contrition, of repentance, the sense of their sinfulness, they close the shutters of their rooms and create an atmosphere of darkness all around them. Try this for yourself. Or go a step further and light a candle in a very dark room. Then set yourself to pray and see if it makes a difference to your prayer. (Only make sure you do not stare fixedly at the candle lest you go into a mild hypnotic trance.) This, I imagine, is the idea behind candlelight dinner at Christmas; the candlelight affects our mood, it creates an atmosphere, just as does the silver light of fluorescent tubelights. Notice the effect that a cloudy day has on you, and a bright day after the rains when all is fresh and alive, and you will understand that all these "material" things affect us very profoundly indeed; they affect our emotional states. Many of the saints drew rich spiritual benefit from them.

Praying in the Same Place: "Holy" Places

I am now going to suggest something that will seem strange to those of you who have not experienced it. I suggest that, as far as possible, you pray either in a place like the ones I have indicated above (exposed to the beauties of nature) or in some "holy" place. What do I mean by a "holy" place? I mean a place reserved for prayer, a church or chapel or prayer room. If this is not possible, then keep some corner in your room or your house for prayer and pray every day there. The place will develop a sacred character and, after a while, you will notice that it is easier to pray there than in another place.

Gradually you will develop what I might call a sense for holy places. You will notice how easy it is to pray in places that have been sanctified by the presence and the prayers of holy people, and you will understand the reason behind pilgrimages to holy places. I know people who are able to walk into a house and tell with fair accuracy the spiritual state of the community living in the house. They can "feel it in the atmosphere." I found this hard to believe myself, but I have too much evidence of it to doubt it any longer now.

I once made a retreat under a Buddhist master who told us that we would probably find it easier to meditate in the prayer hall than in our rooms. I noticed, to my surprise, that this was true. He attributed it to the "good vibrations" in the room, vibrations that had come there as a result of so much prayer that had been offered in that room. I attributed it to autosuggestion, to the fact that the master had suggested it. When I myself conducted a similar retreat for a large group of Jesuits, I was careful not to make any suggestion with regard to the place of prayer. To my surprise, many of them began to tell me on their own that they found it much easier to meditate, to find peace and tranquillity, in the chapel than in their rooms! Eventually I was told by a Jesuit confrere who happened to be giving a retreat in another place that a sannyasi (a Hindu holy man) living nearby once said to him, after the retreat, "What were you doing in your house between nine and ten each night? From my house I could sense a very great increase of good vibrations." The Jesuit retreat master was surprised: each night between nine and ten all the retreatants gathered together in the chapel for an hour of adoration before the Blessed Sacrament. How had this sannyasi sensed it across the street when no one had told him what was going on?

This leads me to another point. Many people have a charism for praying before the Blessed Sacrament. Somehow when they are in the presence of the Eucharist their prayer comes alive. We hear of saints who had this charism to such an intense degree that they were able to tell, as if by instinct, if the Blessed Sacrament were preserved in a place or not, even though there were no external signs by which they could tell; or they could even tell the difference between a consecrated host and an unconsecrated one merely from this instinct they had for the Blessed Sacrament. Your charism may not be as strong as theirs, but it may be strong enough for you to have noticed that it does make a difference to your prayer when you pray before the Blessed Sacrament. If this is so, then I suggest that you "exploit" this charism, that you do not let it die, because it will bring you many spiritual blessings. Pray before the Blessed Sacrament whenever you can.

One final remark on this subject of the place of prayer: No matter where you pray, make sure the place is clean. I once read a Buddhist book on meditation where concrete and detailed instructions were given on preparation of the place of meditation: Sweep the place clean, the book said, then mop it; place a spotlessly clean sheet on it; then take a bath to purify your body, wear light clothing that is also spotlessly clean; light a pair of incense sticks to give the place a fragrant atmosphere. Then begin your meditation. Very good advice, indeed. Have you noticed what a difference it makes to your devotion to have the Eucharist celebrated at an altar that is shabby, to have the priest wear shoddy vestments and to notice that the altar linen is soiled? Change all of that (all you need is a couple of assistants) and you will be surprised at the transformation! Scrub everything clean: the altar, the floor, the sacred vessels, the candlesticks. Use snow white linen on the altar and simple, but attractive vestments for the priest—it is as if you have been interiorly renewed!

I remember walking into a little Buddhist shrine somewhere in the Himalayas. There were little silver bowls of varying size placed before an image of the Buddha, all of them filled with water. The bowls were bright and sparkling and the water crystal clear and the mere sight of them did something to me and does something to me even today when I remember them. They somehow put me into the presence of God.

Pay attention, then, to the place where you worship. It will not be long before you notice the beneficial results of this in your prayer.

Aids to Prayer: Time

I told you in a previous conference that it is only with a good deal of reluctance that most of us accept the fact of our dependence on matter and act accordingly. Matter seemingly puts limits to us; it seems to curb our freedom, and so we do not find it pleasant to have to choose a place for prayer that will be conducive to prayer. (Why can't we be beings who can pray just anywhere without having to bother about the place of prayer?) We do not find it pleasant to seek help from our bodies, to search for postures conducive to prayer. (Why not any posture at all? Why do we have to depend on our bodies?)

There is perhaps no dependence that we accept more reluctantly than our dependence on time. How wonderful it would be if we did not need time for prayer; if we could compress all our prayer into one compact minute and have done with it. There are so many, many things to do—books to read, work to finish, people to meet. For most of us the twenty-four hours of each day are just not enough for all the things we have to do. And so it does seem a great pity that we have to expend a great deal of this precious time in prayer. If only there were some way of having Instant Prayer, the way we have Instant Coffee and Instant Tea! Or suppose we just said that everything we do is a prayer? That might be an easier way of getting around the difficulty.

But as the months and the years roll by we know that this formula simply doesn't work. There is no such thing as Instant Prayer any more than there is such a thing as Instant Relationship. If you want to build a deep and lasting relationship with someone, you have to be ready to invest lots and lots of time in it. That is the way it is with prayer, which, after all, is a relationship with God. As the years pass we also realize that we have fooled ourselves when we lulled ourselves into believing that everything we do is a prayer. We would have been more accurate if we had said that everything we do *ought* to be a prayer. But, alas, what ought to be, and what actually is a reality in the lives of many saintly prayerful people, is not yet a reality for us. We had just not reached that depth of intimate communion with God necessary for making our every action a prayer, before we embarked upon this everything-is-a-prayer program.

Perhaps it is safe to say that the two biggest obstacles to prayer for modern human beings are (1) nervous tension, which makes it impossible for them to be still and (2) lack of time. Too many pressing demands are made on our time and we are, unfortunately, all too inclined to feel that prayer is a waste of time, chiefly when it does not yield immediate results that are perceptible to mind and heart and senses.

Rhythm of Prayer: Kairos Versus Chronos

Unless you have a very special gift of prayer from the Lord, a gift that, in my experience, is very rarely given to people, you are going to have to invest a great deal of time in prayer if you desire to make progress in it and to deepen your relationship with God. Learning to pray is just like learning any other art or skill. It calls for much, much practice, and a great deal of time and patience. Because you are up today and down tomorrow, you feel you have made a great breakthrough today and tomorrow you wonder if you aren't right back in square one. Finally, learning to pray calls for regular, even daily, exercise. If you are learning to play tennis or the violin it will never do to invest a lot of time in it one day and then neglect it for the next; it will never do to "play when you feel like it." You have to play regularly, whether you feel like it or not, if your hands and your whole body are going to get adjusted to the racquet or the musical instrument and if you are to develop the sixth sense that makes you a virtuoso. If you practice in fits and starts you might as well not set out at all to master the art; you are just wasting all the time that you invest in it so irregularly. Praying when you "feel like it" is just as bad as playing when you feel like it—if your aim is to master the art, that is. The less you pray the worse it gets.

There used to be a theory some ten years ago that was marketed under the label of "Rhythm of prayer." In my opinion it did a lot of harm—it certainly did some harm to my own prayer life—and, even though it has lost a considerable portion of the popularity it enjoyed among priests and religious a decade ago, I feel it is sufficiently alive and flourishing to continue to do much harm. I should therefore like to explain it and refute it. Mind you, I am not against every theory that goes under the rhythm-of-prayer title. It is just the type that I am about to explain that I am against.

According to this theory, different people are differently constituted where prayer is concerned, just as different people are differently constituted where physical exercises are concerned. There is no doubt that everybody, to keep healthy, needs a certain amount of physical exercise. But some need more and others need less. Some need to take their exercise daily. Others don't. They take it at irregular intervals when the body feels the need of it. Regular exercise, doing exercise according to a timetable, seems as irrational (though perhaps not so harmful) as eating according to a prefixed timetable. You eat when you are hungry. To act otherwise is both irrational and harmful.

And so it is with prayer. There is no doubt that prayer needs time. The question is how much time, and what time. Should it be a lengthy period each time, like a full hour or more? Should it be regular, like once a day or even more than once a day? This would be to pray according to the chronometer and not according to the movement of grace and one's own spiritual needs. There are two words to express time in Greek: *chronos*, meaning the quantity of time—minutes, seconds, hours—and *kairos*, meaning the hour of grace, not the hour according to the clock. This is the sense in which Jesus uses the word when he speaks of his "time" or his "hour." He is talking of his kairos, the divinely appointed time, the hour of grace. Well, says this theory, let us pray, not according to a pre-fixed time-table but according to our own personal kairos. Let us search for the time of grace, be alert to the call of God to pray and to our own spiritual needs and, when the call comes, or the need is felt, then let us pray and give all the time necessary to it until the need is satisfied or the divine call has been answered.

The theory is, indeed, a very attractive one because it seems so reasonable. I am sorry to say I was converted to it myself and lived it out for a couple of years—with not a little harm to my prayer life. And there is no one I know of, among the many, many priests and religious I have directed, who has profited from living by this theory. Let me tell you why.

First of all, as I said above, the less you pray the worse it gets. You keep putting it off for some other time. There are dozens of things that are clamoring for your time and attention, there are all sorts of emergencies, urgent situations, crises, and it isn't long before you realize that it is ages since you have prayed for any length of time, except, perhaps, for the Mass or some liturgical function. You gradually begin to lose your appetite for prayer; your "prayer muscles" or your "prayer faculties" get atrophied, so to speak, and except in moments of distress when you need God's help desperately, you begin to live pretty much without any prayer. I claim that the human being is essentially a praying animal. If we could quieten the noise within ourselves, if we could be helped to come home to ourselves, prayer would rise up spontaneously within our hearts. However, human beings also carry within themselves a deep-seated reluctance to pray. Frequently we resolve to pray, to come home to ourselves, to present ourselves before our God, but we experience a resistance within ourselves—a barely perceptible voice that calls us away. How often have we not experienced this when, having overcome the voice and betaken ourselves to prayer, we are tempted repeatedly to give it up, to leave the chapel or the place of prayer, to abandon this unfamiliar world into which we are venturing and to return to the familiar sights and sounds and occupations of our daily routine of the world in which we are more at home?

This leads me to my second argument against the pray-when-you-feel-called-to theory. I have just said that the danger in this is that you feel the call less and less; you become less sensitive to it. It is another call, the call away from prayer that keeps occupying your consciousness. In his Spiritual Exercises St. Ignatius speaks of this voice calling us away from prayer as one of the standard experiences of those who are giving themselves to God and to a life of prayer. There are consoling periods, he says, when it is very easy and delightful to pray. But then come periods of what he calls "desolation" when it becomes exceedingly difficult to pray. One loses one's appetite for prayer. One may even feel disgusted with it. When this happens, says Ignatius, far from giving in to this and abandoning prayer to return to it when we are in a better mood, we are to consider this as an attack of the evil one and we are to resist it with courage (a) by not cutting down in the least the time we have allotted to prayer (b) by making no change whatsoever in our prayer timetable and finally, (c) by even adding a little extra time to the time we had fixed for prayer. This last advice generally proves to be extremely beneficial even psychologically because when you know that any inclination to desist from prayer will be given in to, you are likely to produce more and more of these inclinations, albeit unconsciously; whereas when the inclination is met with vigor and with an increased amount of time given to prayer, it somehow tends to go away!

This whole approach of Ignatius is, of course, diametrically opposed to the theory I am at present refuting. And experience itself will show you the wisdom of this approach and the rich spiritual benefits it brings. How often people have told me that they have struggled through their prayer, fighting distractions, resisting the temptation to get up and go away, ignoring the persistent voice that tells them they are wasting their time, shoring up their determination to stick it out for the whole time they had fixed to give to prayer, and then, mysteriously, toward the end of that time things have changed completely, and they have been flooded with light, grace, and love of God. If they had gone away on the understanding that this was not their "kairos" they would have missed the many graces that God had kept for them at the end of their prayer, as a reward for their struggle and their fidelity.

I am reminded now of a Jesuit seminarian who was given a deep experience of Christ one day, an experience that had a decisive effect on his spiritual life, when he did just that—he resisted the temptation to give in to disgust and distractions and to quit praying. He went into the chapel one evening to fulfil his daily "duty" of giving a full hour to prayer. After ten minutes he began to experience what he had experienced very frequently, nearly always, each time he went to pray—a strong urge to get up and go away. He resisted the urge that day, not so much from any very spiritual motive as from the purely practical consideration that he had nothing very particular to do that particular hour and he might just as well waste it in the chapel as in his room. So he stuck it out. And ten minutes before the prayer was to end, it happened. Christ came into his life and into his consciousness in a way he had never come before, filling this man's heart and the whole of his being with the awareness of Christ's consoling presence. Here was one man who was deeply grateful that he did not follow what he might have thought was his "rhythm of prayer." And there are many, many more like him. I am fairly certain that all of you who are reading this are like this too. Don't take my word for it; test it out for a period of six months and see if it doesn't prove true for you too.

There is a third and final reason I have against the prayer-rhythm theory and it is this: When a person has made some progress in his prayer life he or she is likely to reach what authors call the Prayer of Faith. This is a form of prayer in which you experience no sensible consolation in general. For example: you generally have a great appetite for prayer, but the moment you go to pray you feel as if you are in a blank, as if you are wasting your time; and you are generally tempted to stop you prayer forthwith and put it off for some other time. Now it is of vital importance that you *not* stop praying, that you continue to invest time in prayer at this stage even though you feel you are wasting your time. What is happening, even though you may not know it, is that you are gradually getting adjusted to another kind of consolation that at the moment only seems like dryness, your spiritual eyes are learning painfully to discern light where now there appears superficially to be only darkness; in other words, you are acquiring new tastes in the matter of prayer. If you were to follow the pray-when-you-feel-called-to-it theory the danger is that you will feel no call whatsoever to pray or, more accurately, feel the call but lose all appetite for prayer the moment you give in to the call; and then, just when you are making progress in the art of prayer, when you are rising to a new and higher level of prayer, you are likely to give it up.

I shall have much more to say about the last two reasons—the necessity and wisdom of praying more rather than less—when we are in spiritual desolation, and about the whole matter of the Prayer of Faith, so I shall content myself with just stating them here as a kind of refutation of the theory I propounded above, and have you wait for a fuller development of these topics in later conferences. There is one point, however, somewhat linked with the matter of the Prayer of Faith, that I want to underscore before passing on to another point. And it is this: truly spiritual people have a nearly habitual desire for prayer. They long to be away from everything and to commune in silence with God, to get in touch with the Infinite, the Eternal, the Ground of their Being, which is our Father, the source of all our life and our well-being and our strength. There isn't a single saint I know of who did not feel this constant urge, this compelling drive, the near-habitual appetite for prayer. Not that they gave in to the drive! No, many of them were too busy doing the work God had allotted them to have the time to satisfy this urge fully. But the urge persisted, creating a kind of holy tension in them, so that when they were at prayer they would feel a longing to be up and about doing great things for Christ, and when they were working for Christ they would be longing to be away from everything and to be with Him alone. St. Paul expressed this tension well in another context, when talking not of prayer, but of his dying and being with the Lord in heaven. He says to the Philippians:

> For to me life is Christ, and death gain; but what if my living
> on in the body may serve some good purpose? Which then am
> I to choose? I cannot tell. I am torn two ways: what I should
> like is to depart and be with Christ; that is better by far; but for
> your sake there is greater need for me to stay on in the body.
>
> Philippians 1:1–25

Paul was an extremely active man, deeply involved in his work and in the life of his early Churches; yet he felt this tension between continuing to work for them and being away with Christ.

The same may be said of other very active men like Francis Xavier or John Vianney, who was constantly having to resist the temptation to run away from his parish and become a hermit so that he could spend all his time with God. This intense desire to be away and alone with God makes the apostle's whole life and activity a prayer, and he is constantly surrounded and steeped in an atmosphere of prayer. Mahatma Gandhi remarked that it was his experience that he could easily live for days on end without eating a single morsel of food, but he could not live for a single minute without prayer. If he were deprived of prayer for even a minute, he said, he would go mad, given the type of life he was leading.

Perhaps that is the reason why we ourselves do not feel this constant hunger for prayer and so fall victim to theories like the one I mentioned above. We are not living the radical lives the Gospels challenge us to live and so we do not feel the constant need for the nourishment and support and vigor and life that only prayer can give us. We are not constantly hungry for prayer. In fact, we feel this hunger very rarely because we have so many things—worldly interests, joys and appetites, even problems and worries—with which to crowd our minds and our consciousness. We are too full of these distractions to sense the great void in our hearts and the great need we have of God to fill that void.

ABOUT THE AUTHOR

Anthony de Mello (1931–1987) is the bestselling author of *Sadhana: A Way to God*, with over a million copies in print. A native and lifelong resident of India, he frequently traveled to Europe and the United States to study and teach. His books have been translated into more than thirty-five languages.

27300023R00121

Made in the USA
Lexington, KY
11 November 2013